"Susan Phillips's *The Cultivated Life* is
Her insightful and sophisticated analy\:
retical and practical in profound and co\
theologian and biblical interpreter, a wis\   _____or, and
one grounded in the common-sense parti\   __\ and complexities of human
experience and history makes her work an extraordinary contribution in so
many arenas of pastoral and theological practice. The breadth of her sources
and insights—from literature, psychology, philosophy, theology, ecumenical
and religious history, and personal history, among others—make this a must-
read for scholars, students and practitioners alike. Phillips's style is accessible,
engaging and invitational. . . . I recommend Susan Phillips's book with great
enthusiasm for all audiences—for all who are searching."
James A. Donahue, president, Saint Mary's College of California

"*The Cultivated Life* is filled with gifts of a generous, transparent spirit. Reading
this insightful book and reflecting on its profound questions invite us to taste
the life Susan Phillips lives. . . . When I reached the end of *The Cultivated Life*
I returned to the beginning to soak in the words, insights and prayers that
arose. Thank you, Susan, for giving us a glimpse of wholeness by offering gifts
of spiritual direction through your writing."
Jeannette A. Bakke, author of *Holy Invitations*

"Susan Phillips tells great stories and uses vivid word pictures. Her contrast
between circus and garden reveals deep truths about the overstimulation in
our daily lives and Jesus' invitation to cultivate a restful and focused life rooted
in him. Cultivation implies habits and discipline, and Susan winsomely invites us into new patterns of living. A garden implies lush green leaves and
fruitful bounty, and Susan guides our paths into joy and rest. Come into the
garden with Jesus and journey into abundant life."
Lynne M. Baab, author of *The Power of Listening* and *Sabbath Keeping*

"The most basic human question in daily living is not so much 'what?' but 'how?'
Just check the magazine covers in the check-out line. Articles promise to tell
us how to lose weight, how to get rich, how to be sexy. But what if you've lived
enough to know that life is about more than health, wealth and a good time?
This is a book for people who are interested in the how of a life that's really
life. Would that it could be front-and-center in every check-out line."
Jonathan Wilson-Hartgrove, author of *Strangers at My Door*

"Susan Phillips can write this book because she lives it. For three decades and more, I have observed the choices she makes to cultivate life and this has been the hallmark of her story. This book is a deep and magnanimous invitation to live in such a way that the flourishing for which we are made can become our experience. Let the grounded welcome she extends and encourages lead us through the circus towards life itself."
Mark Labberton, president of Fuller Theological Seminary

"*The Cultivated Life* reads like the cool evening breeze at the end of a blazing hot day in the desert.... It is also a prophetic clarion call—a warning to a generation trapped in the meaningless rat-race of twenty-first-century existence, suffocated by the demands of addictive consumerism, obsessed with the lifeless toys of modernity, while the breath of heaven who is only a prayer away eagerly waits to share with us the real joys of living. This book is a timely gift to the community of faith to be treasured and shared. More than that, this is essential survival reading for every true pilgrim seeking after the pearl of great price."
Ivan Satyavrata, senior pastor, Assembly of God Church, Kolkata, India

"We all struggle in the circus-like culture of contemporary society, which often causes difficulties in attention and healthy attachment in the midst of yearning for the spiritual life. Susan Phillips provides us with ways to cultivate the contemplative life by examining spiritual practices within the Christian tradition such as spiritual direction, *lectio divina*, listening and friendship. I believe the author's use of stories—stories that have emerged from her practice of attentive listening—will affect readers deeply."
Jung Eun Sophia Park, assistant professor of religious studies and philosophy, Holy Names University

THE CULTIVATED *Life*

FROM CEASELESS STRIVING TO RECEIVING JOY

SUSAN S. PHILLIPS

FOREWORD BY EUGENE H. PETERSON

IVP Books

An imprint of InterVarsity Press
Downers Grove, Illinois

InterVarsity Press
P.O. Box 1400, Downers Grove, IL 60515-1426
ivpress.com
email@ivpress.com

InterVarsity Press® is the book-publishing division of InterVarsity Christian Fellowship/USA®, a movement of students and faculty active on campus at hundreds of universities, colleges and schools of nursing in the United States of America, and a member movement of the International Fellowship of Evangelical Students. For information about local and regional activities, visit intervarsity.org.

Scripture quotations, unless otherwise noted, are from the New Revised Standard Version of the Bible, copyright 1989 by the Division of Christian Education of the National Council of the Churches of Christ in the USA. Used by permission. All rights reserved.

While any stories in this book are true, some names and identifying information may have been changed to protect the privacy of individuals.

Material taken and adapted from "Garden or Circus? Christian Care in the Face of Contemporary Pressures" that appeared in Transformation vol. 22, no. 3 is used by permission.

Material taken and adapted from "Stop in the Name of Love! The Radical Practice of Sabbath-Keeping" that appeared in Crux vol. 47, no. 3 is used by permission.

Cover design: Cindy Kiple
Interior design: Beth McGill

Images: green vine plant: Old man's beard or Traveller's Joy—Clematis vitalba (Vitis nigra), Leonhard Fuchs, Biblioteca Nazionale, Turin, Italy / De Agostini Picture Library / Bridgeman Images.
vintage frames: © Electric_Crayon/iStockphoto

ISBN 978-0-8308-3598-0 (print)
ISBN 978-0-8308-9766-7 (digital)

Printed in the United States of America ∞

 As a member of the Green Press Initiative, InterVarsity Press is committed to protecting the environment and to the responsible use of natural resources. To learn more, visit greenpressinitiative.org.

Library of Congress Cataloging-in-Publication Data

Phillips, Susan (Susan S.)
  The cultivated life : from ceaseless striving to receiving joy / Susan S. Phillips ; foreword by Eugene H. Peterson.
      pages cm
  Includes bibliographical references and index.
  ISBN 978-0-8308-3598-0 (pbk. : alk. paper)
  1. Spiritual life--Christianity. 2. Christianity and culture. I. Title.
  BV4501.3.P495 2015
  248.4--dc23
                                                                                2015013544

| P | 21 | 20 | 19 | 18 | 17 | 16 | 15 | 14 | 13 | 12 | 11 | 10 | 9 | 8 | 7 | 6 | 5 | 4 | 3 | 2 | 1 |
| Y | 33 | 32 | 31 | 30 | 29 | 28 | 27 | 26 | 25 | 24 | 23 | 22 | 21 | 20 | 19 | 18 | 17 | 16 | 15 |

To my parents,

whose lives of significant soil so enriched my life,

and to Steve, Andrew and Peter,

who, by God's grace, continue to cultivate it.

CONTENTS

Foreword

SUSAN PHILLIPS HAS BEEN FOR MANY YEARS my writer of choice in matters of spiritual direction and maturing a robust Christian life. Her earlier work *Candlelight: Illuminating the Art of Spiritual Direction* is the book that I most often refer to others. This latest offering continues to develop perceptions and insights that keep our attention and participating obedience focused and alert and listening—maybe *mostly* listening.

One of the strengths of her imagination is her skill in using metaphors, words that occur at the intersection of the visible and invisible. This is especially necessary when we take seriously the life of faith in the circumstances of ordinary day-by-day living, circumstances in which the visible and invisible are continuously contiguous. Jesus used a lot of metaphors. A metaphor is literally a lie. One of Jesus' well-known metaphors is "You are the salt of the earth." It requires an imagination to comprehend it. I know that I am not salt, neither are you salt. I do not sprinkle myself on my eggs at breakfast. Nor can I enter a laboratory and put myself under a microscope and analyze the chemical parts of my body to find out what I am made of. But even a child knows that Jesus is not saying anything about what we look like or how I taste or what a surgeon might find if she was performing open-heart surgery. With metaphors, literal gets us nowhere.

The two prominent metaphors around which this book is organized are cultivation and circus. *Cultivation* is an agricultural metaphor: working the soil to prepare it to grow something useful—planting and watering seeds, weeding and pruning, harvesting. Everyone knows what is involved in cultivation; when it is used to refer to our lives, it needs neither explanation nor definition. *Circus* is a social metaphor that brings to mind the complexity of activity in a three-ring setting under the big tent, everything going on at once. A circus is the place to see performers doing funny things, dangerous things, clowns and trapeze artists, lion tamers and people shot out of a cannon—all of this without our participation. It turns out to be a powerful metaphor to bring to mind the mindless absorption in entertainment and business that has infiltrated our daily lives, but almost entirely as spectators.

In an age of self-absorption, *cultivation* is a metaphor that can keep us aware that we are not merely individuals defined by what we consume or possess or do but by our relationships, our values and our faith, all of which require attentiveness. In an age of distraction that proliferates with every new technical device, the *circus* metaphor keeps us aware of the necessity of making alert discernments that will keep us from depending on entertainment and frenzy to compensate for an inner emptiness.

This is a book written specifically for those of us who are assigned the task of developing an imagination for living the Christian faith with insight and skill in and for a society that is disconnected from the biblical revelation and the Jesus incarnation. But it is equally useful for all of us who are committed to following Jesus with our families and coworkers and neighbors.

When some of our ancient Israelite predecessors in this life of faith were being led by Moses in the wilderness, they noticed that two of their neighbors were "prophesying" (preaching and teaching) without authorization, and they complained to Moses that "Eldad and Medad are prophesying in the camp." Moses famously replied, "Would that all the Lord's people were prophets" (Numbers 11:26-29). The same, I think, might be said of spiritual directors and spiritual friends.

....

In addition to skill in using metaphors, another conspicuous feature of this book is the use of personal names and stories in the narration. Eugen Rosenstock-Huessy, the impressive language scholar of an earlier generation, held that "names are . . . the most important grammatical form in language, any language." All other parts of speech are, or can be, lifeless, dealing objectively with what is. But "names are vehicles of spirit: they reveal social functions; separate people and unite them."[1]

Susan Phillips includes herself in the naming. Her word for it is *self-implicating*—she herself is implicated in what she is writing in relation to others and God. One of the delights in reading this book is that we come into the presence of a person who is not just giving us information but has been, all the time she is writing, living what she is writing: "The hope behind this book is that as you read about a spirituality of cultivation (while immersed in a circus of distractions) you will be formed by God's grace, as I have been formed while I have written it. My own experience is written into the book, and writing the book has been part of God's cultivation of my life."

There is also this: names are seeds. When they germinate they become stories. A seed that is not buried in the ground remains nothing but a seed. But planted it becomes, in Jesus' self-prophecy, "much fruit" (John 12:24). This was anticipated half a millennium earlier in the prophet Isaiah's vision of the "holy seed" (Isaiah 6:13) embedded in the stump of the devastated Jerusalem temple that became the "branch" that turned out to be Jesus Christ (Isaiah 11:1).

Life has a story shape. The life of the Spirit is necessarily relational, always relational. The names develop into stories. The most adequate rendering of the way things are is through storytelling. It is the least specialized and most comprehensive form of language. Everything and anything can be put into the story. And from the moment it is in the story it develops meaning, participates in plot, becomes, somehow or other, significant. The entire biblical revelation comes to us in the form of story. Nothing less than story is adequate to the largeness and intricacy of the truth of creation and redemption.

Our biblical ancestors in the faith were magnificent storytellers. The stories they told reverberate down through the corridors of worshiping communities and resonate in our hearts as sharply in tune with reality as when they were first told. They map the country of our humanity, show its contours, reveal its dimensions. Mostly what they show is that to be human means to deal with God. And that everything we encounter and experience—birth and death, hunger and thirst, money and weapons, weather and mountains, friendship and betrayal, marriage and adultery, every nuance and detail of it—deals with God.

It is enormously significant that stories and storytelling are given such a prominent role in revealing God and God's ways to us. Young and old love stories. Literate and illiterate alike tell and listen to stories. Neither stupidity nor sophistication puts us out of the magnetic field of story. The only serious rivals to story in terms of accessibility and attraction are song and poetry, and there are plenty of these also in our Scriptures. When it came time for Matthew, Mark, Luke and John to give their witness, mostly they had Jesus telling stories, and then he *became* the Story.

There is another reason for the appropriateness of story as a major means of bringing us God's Word. Story doesn't just tell us something and leave it at that—it invites our participation. A good storyteller gathers us into the story. We feel the emotions, get caught up in the plot, identify with the characters, see into the nooks and crannies of life that we had overlooked, realize that there is more to this business of being human than we had yet explored. If the storyteller is good, doors and windows open. Our biblical storytellers were good in both the artistic and the moral sense, as is Dr. Phillips.

One of the characteristic marks of our biblical storytellers is a certain reticence, and the stories told here continue that reticence. There is an austere, spare quality to these stories. They don't tell us too much. They leave a lot of blanks in the narration, an implicit invitation to hear the story ourselves just as we are and find how we fit into it. These are stories that respect our freedom. They don't manipulate, don't force. They show us a spacious world in which God creates and saves and blesses. First through our imagination and then through our faith—imagination and faith are close kin here—they offer us a place in the story, invite us into this large story that takes place under the broad skies of God's purposes, in contrast to the gossipy anecdotes that we cook up in the stuffy closet of the self.

Storytelling that arises between friends working things out in conversation doesn't abstract an episode in life into a moral lesson. Such friends don't use the story as a platform for shouting "God!" at us. They don't bully us with moral cudgels. They gently "story" our seemingly plotless lives and open our ears and eyes to the *real* story, the *real* world, so that we can live in it with all our heart, soul, mind, and strength.

Stories suffer misinterpretation when we don't submit to them simply as stories. We are caught off guard when divine revelation arrives in such ordinary garb and think that it's our job to dress it up in the latest Paris silk gown of theology or outfit it in a sturdy three-piece suit of ethics before we can deal with it. The simple, or not so simple, story is soon, like David outfitted in Saul's armor, so encumbered with moral admonitions, theological constructs and scholarly debates that it can hardly move.

One more caution: It is the devil's own work to take the stories that Jesus told and the ones that we find ourselves telling in conversation and distill them down to a "truth" or a "doctrine" or a "moral" that can be used without bothering with the *way* they are used, the people whose names we know or the local conditions in which we have responsibilities. The devil is a great intellectual; he loves getting us into discussing ideas about good and evil, ideas about God, *especially* ideas about God. He does some of his best work when he gets us so deeply involved in *ideas* about God that we are hardly aware that while we are reading or talking about God, God is actually present to us, and that the people he has placed in our lives to love are right there in front of us. The devil doesn't tell stories.

As you read this wonderful introduction into the world of Christian spirituality, prepare to be blessed with hours of companionship with a friend who is providing generous and wise counsel to many like you who are cultivating a life of Christ-in-you in a "big tent circus" world of "ceaseless striving."

Eugene H. Peterson
Professor Emeritus of Spiritual Theology, Regent College, Vancouver

Introduction

LEAVING THE CIRCUS

Where is the Life we have lost in living?

T. S. ELIOT, CHORUSES FROM *THE ROCK*

*I*N GIANT BILLBOARD LETTERING, a California medical organization implores freeway drivers, "Thrive." A bumper sticker taunts, "Jesus is coming. Look busy." Other cars recommend pacifism, a vegan diet and yoga. Even on a morning commute we are prompted to ask, Where is the Life we have lost in living, and how can we get to it? As the word *thrive* increases in popularity, we want to know how to help our stifled souls grow.

As I listen to people in Christian spirituality classes and in spiritual direction, I hear questions asking "how": How can we fashion flourishing lives from our time-compressed, multi-tasking days? How can we follow Jesus, the Way and the Life, and receive God's joy? How can we participate in the cultivation of our souls in a ceaselessly striving, circus-like culture that pushes us to be performers and spectators? As I move from one meeting to the next, juggling priorities and balancing demands, I, too, wonder how it's possible to orient myself toward God when I am so engaged by the three rings of my calendared life.

Scripture, practices of faithful living and spiritual insights from people around the world and through time offer a treasury of wisdom about the cultivated life, which informs this book. As you read about a spirituality of cultivation, may you sense the pulse of Life in your own life and be refreshed by God's grace, as I have been in writing it.

SEEKING LIFE

Many of us, sounding like T. S. Eliot, ask what has happened to Life—with all its capitalized significance. Recently when speaking at a church retreat, I listened at a coffee break to a middle-aged retreatant who gave voice to the difficulty of finding Life in living. Matt (not his real name, and I quote from memory) said, "I've been a Christian for decades. I try to live the right way, but I'm not sure I've made much progress on the way forward, you know, the way of growth, even flourishing." He shook his head slowly and looked at the floor, not meeting my eyes while continuing to speak.

"I feel, spiritually, the same way I did when I became a Christian as a teenager. I haven't grown, but I'm older," he said, wincing. "I'd like to end well, if you know what I mean. I'm not sure what way of living would make a change, a change to the rut I'm in spiritually. It's not easy to alter my ways."

We stood in a hallway while around us people chatted and snacked. Matt told me how years have flown by: He's built a career, raised a family, and every day juggles balls tossed his way. He has done well and been satisfied with work and family life. My impression was that his days are long and the years far too short.

Matt looked at me tearfully and said, "I want to become more the way God would have me be." Then, immediately turning to the "how" questions, he asked if I could think of any spiritual practices that might help him grow.

Matt yearns for what I call the "cultivated life." He wants to find the Life he's lost in living, and he trusts that Life also seeks him. God cares and has a way for him to be. But in the midst of a good and full life, something important has gone missing. Perhaps it's Matt who has gone missing somehow while going about his "ways" and losing track of God's "way" for him. His longing to grow and flourish was palpable as he spoke of a way of living with God even in the midst of his ways in the world. His willingness to take up the necessary work was evident in his question about spiritual practices. Desire and discipline go hand in hand in soul cultivation, and Matt wants to participate in his becoming.

The longing for a meaningful life also throbs in the hearts of people whose lives are remote from Matt's in many ways, for questions about the cultivated life span generations and cultures. The investigative journalist Katherine Boo listened to teenaged waste-scavengers in a Mumbai slum and reported a conversation between two boys: "Do you ever think when you look at someone, when you listen to someone, does that person really have a life?" Remembering lives that ended tragically, the boy concluded, "Even the person who lives like a dog still has a kind of life."[1] Boo wrote that "something he's come to realize on the roof, leaning out, thinking about what would happen if he leaned too far, was that a boy's life could still matter to himself."[2]

Even in slums people ask the "how" questions about making a life. Another teenager Boo got to know imagines that the substance of a life is like the mixture of two parts hydrogen and one part oxygen, and it can be experienced differently depending on whether it's in a liquid or solid state. He is sure that there are things a boy can do to make the water of his life like ice—to make his life worthy and significant for him as well as for people affected by his life.[3] He trusts that there are ways to find Life in living.

Asking questions like Matt's yet with a life so different from Matt's, this boy too may choose to live a cultivated life, a way that allows for soul flourishing. This is a statement of faith. Boo shows that even in the most impoverished conditions, boys cherish their lives. In fact, a boy hopes that life can be cultivated and decides to participate in his becoming by directing his desire into discipline. However, the circumstances of that boy's life are crushing, and by the book's end he thinks it may not be possible to resist the melting forces of his circumstances. It's remarkable that he's been ice-strong for as long as he has.

WORDS AND WAYS

As a spiritual director, I tune in to words people use when talking about spiritual matters, for many words function as lenses through which we can see more deeply into the human soul. In particular, metaphors and verbal images bridge the gap between the conscious and unconscious in us, serving as vehicles of personal and cultural insight. The boy in the Indian slum hopes to forge a solid, icelike character. In an American suburb, Matt thinks he's in a rut. Both ice and rut are verbal images of things that are real and concrete—H_2O in its solid state and a deep groove in the ground—and illuminate abstract, intangible aspects of life.

Metaphors help us explore "what if" and "how" questions. They shape the stories we tell about ourselves and the world. The boy in the Mumbai slum thought he could be like ice. He could exert discipline and become stronger, move forward in his life and benefit others in doing so. A metaphor inspired him, bridging the gap between desire and discipline, bringing a new lens through which to view his life. The image of ice made from the simple elements of his life engendered hope.

Scholars understand metaphors as "mappings across conceptual domains that structure our reasoning, our experience, and our everyday language."[4] These potent words shape the way we know and how we act. They also enhance our spirituality: "Through metaphor, the vividness, intensity, and meaningfulness of ordinary experience becomes the basis of passionate spirituality."[5] Metaphors breathe life and understanding into our lives of faith by bridging the conscious and unconscious, the immanent and the transcendent. They help us follow what Matt called "God's way" and develop the fortitude the boy called "ice."

Practices shape and are shaped by metaphors. We bow to a monarch and follow a shepherd. Perhaps we take particular actions to get out and stay out of a rut, or we engage in disciplines that keep us ice-hard in a culture that would melt us. The story flows. A self—indeed, a life—is constructed through regular practices, and the practices we engage in are shaped by stories.

IMAGINING CULTIVATION OF OUR LIVES

This book draws on the biblical imagery of cultivation and the narratives that animate it. Human life appears in its rootedness and branching, entailing movements that go up, out and down. Cultivation also entails a cooperative endeavor: we are planted, bear fruit and receive a gardener's care. Through the lens of cultivation, we see our lives taking place in God's garden.

The image of the garden stands in contrast to what many of us experience during our long days and short lives. Matt felt his life had been consumed by demands to perform and achieve. He juggles, puts out fires and climbs the professional ladder. These images come from what I conceive of as the dark side of our contemporary culture: a circus-like environment of fragmented attention and fractured relationships in which we strain to perform or passively view the spectacle of other people performing.

Our times and their technological innovations contain possibilities for spiritual practice that were unimaginable until recently. Alongside those possibilities are obstacles. Driving to work, we listen to podcasted prayers, our attention fragmenting as we simultaneously attune to the sound of traffic and possibly eye a GPS or a smartphone's incoming messages. We are able to join others in prayer through the marvels of technology, yet the same technology creates distance from other people, ourselves and our awareness of God.

Every culture in its own way makes spiritual cultivation possible, and also thwarts it. The assurance, however, is that we are participating with a God who can cultivate our souls wherever we are. The apostle Paul told the sophisticated Athenians that all of us "live and move and have our being" in God (Acts 17:28). All of us—in the suburbs and in the slums.

Soon after reading about the boys in the Mumbai slums, I spent a few weeks visiting development projects and churches in India. Outside Agra my husband Steve and I met a community of people[6] the culture designates as Dalits (which literally means "crushed" and is sometimes rendered "untouchable"). Some of them, though born into that socially outcast status, had heard of the God who calls them "beloved." That God even became a man who walked the earth and was himself crushed.

Among the Dalit Christians, new metaphors and practices sprang from the good news. Lives were transformed. Born into jobs dealing with waste and sewage, these marginalized people now pursue careers and strive to cultivate a better world.

Dalit Christian theologians have written, "Dalits reimagine themselves along positive lines in the service of a new world that frees not just themselves but all those who are imprisoned within the present world disorder."[7] Belovedness begets hope. No longer prisoners of the "present world disorder," they live in the realm of grace, the "assurance of things hoped for" (Hebrews 11:1).

VARIETIES OF CULTIVATION

Our culture generates metaphors, stories and enveloping conditions that shape our lives. While God transcends culture, culture also shapes how we apprehend God. To experience is to encounter or undergo something, and we are always being shaped by our experience, whether or not we're aware of the process. Certain experiences, through impact and frequency, cultivate us in deep ways—like the rutted ways Matt spoke about or the caste-based and crushing experiences of the Dalits. Some cultivation is chosen, some inflicted and some merely sustained. We are always being cultivated.

Today we're living through a communications revolution of unprecedented scope, and a branch of communication studies is called "cultivation theory." Cultivation theorists study how we attend to our culture's media, especially television, "religiously."[8] We believe what we see and devotedly engage in practices of viewing that shape what we know and how we think. Screen media saturate our lives the way religion does some cultures. As of 2010, 51 percent of US households had TVs on most of the time, and children spent between twenty-eight and thirty-two hours a week in front of the screen—nearly full-time employment.[9] Though good may come from media viewing, it cultivates the spectator posture.

Thus we are being cultivated in ways beyond our awareness and choosing. However, this is not a garden-like cultivation conducive to spiritual growth, but rather the cultivation of a dystopian circus milieu in which a few are high-wire performers and most are spectators.

Consider how you are being cultivated. What occupies the hours of your days? What's trending on the media you ingest? With whom do you spend your time, in person and on devices, by

choice or not? Human beings are sensitive, impressionable creatures. Babies cry when they hear another baby crying; adults yawn
contagiously. Our desires, too, are shaped by other people's desires,
possessions and opinions, be those people the Joneses next door
or persons in the media. Where we live shapes our opinions on
public issues, and increasingly we live in a cyberspace broadcast
neighborhood.

The challenge is to choose and participate in our spiritual cultivation within a captivating circus-like culture.

THE CIRCUS AROUND US

My awareness of my own circus living began a few years into the new
millennium. Feeling a bit stagnant in my spiritual life and seeking
ways to participate more conscientiously in God's cultivation of my
soul, I undertook the Spiritual Exercises of St. Ignatius in the thirty-
week format under the guidance of my spiritual director.

The Exercises were developed more than three hundred years
ago by Ignatius of Loyola as a devotional practice for those in his
religious community, and they are now undertaken by Christians
from many traditions. Engaging in the daily prayer practice was a
commitment I made in a year full of challenging work and family
responsibilities. I hoped the prayers and the accompaniment of my
spiritual director would provide spiritual rootedness during a
windy season in my life.

Praying each morning with biblical passages about Jesus' life
directed my attention to what moved my heart toward God (con-
solation) and away from God (desolation) and, at the same time,
toward and away from my deepest self and other people. Over the
nine months of daily, hour-long prayers, I noticed that my heart
could pivot in an instance. After my morning prayer, while driving
to work in traffic and the narrative of radio news, I'd be swept up

in the rush of the world. Before even registering the change, I would be angry with a slow driver blocking my progress or be vaguely anxious because of a financial news report containing little relevance to my life. Alienation from God, myself and people in my life set in quickly, like a rigor mortis of my soul that had so recently been tenderized by prayer.

I felt I breathed more shallowly while my attention scanned all it encountered. Then, remembering Jesus' life and the time I'd spent in prayer, I breathed more deeply and reoriented myself toward God. I came to think of myself as moving between the garden of God's grace and the circus of the culture, seeing evidence of those metaphorical domains around and within me.

During that year I was invited to speak to clergy and theological educators who had traveled to Oxford, England, for a respite from daily ministry and an opportunity to pursue graduate study before returning to their homes in Africa, Asia, Latin America and Eastern Europe.[10] Drawing on what I was experiencing in the Spiritual Exercises, I spoke about garden living and how it contrasts with our culture's circus living. A few people responded by accusing the church in North America, and me as its representative, of doing nothing to impede or protest the international export of what I was calling "the circus." Some expressed gratitude for the North's sharing of resources and technologies, but many in the audience argued that the benefits of globalization came with toxic anti-Christian side effects, such as the destruction of communities, the mindless speeding up of life and the hegemony of materialistic values.

One religious leader from Africa asked, "What do you in the American church do to stop the distribution of music and films that destroy families and basic human civility?" Another asked, "Can you offer an alternative to the hyped-up, production-style worship that gets broadcast from your country?" Those questions have stayed with me, and I've been asked similar questions since then. What *does* the global North cultivate in other countries through the worldwide dissemination of our circus-like culture—secular and religious—and what is the responsibility of people of faith?

During that time in England I reflected on my own country, which in recent years had been experiencing the circus of 24/7 media broadcasts of wars, domestic partisan battles, financial crises and disasters of many varieties. We do not live with the daily privations familiar to those with whom I conversed in England, but stress streams into American homes as we are presented with threats we cannot predict, control or objectively assess. It's a spectacle, and we, more affluent than much of the world, its anxious spectators.

Anxieties are amplified by our collective buzz. Poet Christian Wiman claims this anxiety is "consuming everyone." When he spends time with other people, he can be left "with the uneasy feeling that my own private anxieties have actually increased" and been "increased by the reinforcement of my loneliness within a collective context."[11]

We're anxious in a lonely crowd, and we're also envious. No longer do we compare ourselves only to our neighbor, but we evaluate our lives in comparison to people viewed on broadcast and social media. As we sit in the seats of our culture's circus, the lives of the rich and famous are in full electronic view, and so are the triumphs of Facebook "friends." To get ahead we perform by juggling and balancing, launching and pounding. Then we assume the spectator posture and veg out, channel surf and quell our anxious striving by ingesting whatever helps us turn off, zone out and graze. The circus is the antithesis of the life-generating and cultivated garden.

CIRCUS TALK

Cultivation metaphors continue to abound, even while we swim in circus imagery. Listen to some circus talk I've heard recently. A young man said, "I can't keep up. It feels like life is passing me by. I need to pedal faster." A mother with a job outside the home lamented, "It feels like I'm living my life in the bleachers, never in the center ring. Yet I work nonstop, all the time, day and night. I even clear emails in the bathroom when I get up in the middle of the night." Both seek a work-life balance yet feel they're juggling so many things that the balls keep dropping. We balance and we juggle.

People speak about achievement in circus language: "He's a star, a high-flyer. He rocketed to the top fast. I hope he doesn't crash and burn." An optimist said, "I want to be a player, score, grab the gold ring. Then I can coast."

We also experience the opposite pole, depletion: "I jumped through too many hoops today at work. I've hit the wall. Let's veg out." And "I feel like a slug, a slacker. I'm sleeping my life away. I need to get my life on track." Speaking of a friend, a woman confidently declared, "She'll be okay. She's working with a net. Her husband's in the big leagues, and so long as she keeps her meds up, she's fine."

People long for something different, possibly the garden: "I feel anesthetized. I need to get out of Dodge so I can know who I am again and be able to hear God." Poignantly, a young father confided, "I have no life, no time for me. I get to work in the dark, having dropped the baby at daycare, try to catch the balls thrown at me all day, then pick up my older kid and arrive home to my wife and baby in the dark again. I don't see my yard in daylight during the week."

There are physical sensations, or the lack of them, associated with the circus experiences of "vegging out," "pedaling faster" and "jumping through hoops." As we're thrown into the shallow places of performing and spectating, we are bereft of feeling and sensation (*an-esthetic* = without feeling) in both circus positions. Yet people long to see, hear and feel.

The blight of circus living has also infiltrated the church. Strategic plans are launched, programs rolled out, emails blasted to the whole congregation, and church staff members often claim—with a triumphant lament—to "work without margins." Busyness has become a badge of significance, albeit a heavy one. A devoted pastor told me about archiving ten thousand emails from the previous six months and needing to clear fifty unheard voicemails in a day, skimming through them quickly to see if any mentioned death. Websites offer e-devotionals for meditation on the run. Clients arrive for spiritual direction and line up on my desk their multiple smartphones, which blink and beep.

While bumper stickers caution, "Jesus is coming. Look busy," a pastor preaches to the congregation that for Lent he will fast from cell phone use; then, driving away from the church, he speed-dials another pastor. While I was editing a document in the lobby of my gym, a client walked past me and said, "Hi, Susan. Always working?" We complain about the circus even while participating in its production.

Within our present world disorder of circus living, faith invites us to see, live and tell the story of the tended garden.

CULTIVATION IN THE "CIRCUS"

Although God offers us cultivated lives, the performer's frenzy disrupts the steady pace of fruition, and the spectator is anesthetized against the sensory richness of the garden. Both features of the circus interfere with cultivation.

Circus living also works against the illumination that story brings. In the circus the focus is on heroic feats rather than the development of persons and relationships. Similarly, in the presentism of our culture, what's significant is what you've done lately and, perhaps, posted. The rapid movement from one spectacle to another allows no time to reflect and explore. One snapshot event or image on a screen succeeds the other, mesmerizing but not cohering as a narrative. No journey is undertaken, nothing is planted and grown. There is no history in the circus.

Circuses as entertainment businesses have a place in our culture and form their own special communities of coworkers. People enjoy time at the circus with family and friends. But the dominance of circus-like performing and spectating postures in everyday life is a calamity. Alternating between those stances takes a toll on us all, personally and relationally, culturally and spiritually. Self-awareness and compassion fade in the glare of the footlights and the shadow of the bleachers. What story are we living in the three rings of the marketplace, workplace and cyberspace?

As people seek to leave the circus and enter the space of spiritual direction, I catch glimpses of the banners they trail from their days. Then, as we attend to the Holy, the pressures and roles of the circus fade. The flame of the candle that I light in each meeting flickers as souls stir. Stories emerge as people reconnect with their senses and feelings. Time stretches, allowing depths to be plumbed, and hearts open to God and to other people.

After offering a closing prayer, I watch people daub tear streaks from their faces or reluctantly hoist briefcases for a return to the fray. Often they stand for a few moments inside my office before they exit, and I wait with them, not opening the door until I see the other take a bracing breath, stand straight and nod a readiness to sally forth. Some faces look softer, bodies less tense. Spiritual practices like spiritual direction help us find the manna and living water that souls crave, and people look nourished as they leave.

THE GARDEN WITHIN THE CIRCUS: AN ILLUSTRATION

Though we all increasingly live in the circus-like culture of the contemporary world, some of us are better able than others to escape it. Certain people have more choice about the circumstances of their work, and some of us can take time for occasional retreats and vacations. Yet Scripture offers the garden to all, affirming that each one of us can be a watered garden (Isaiah 58:11) and a branch in the vine the gardener tends (John 15:1). It would be foolish and cruel to hold up a standard of spiritual living that is inaccessible to most people, so this book offers stories from people around the world who live in challenging circumstances yet are cultivating spiritual gardens.

In 2006 I read a newspaper article about Chinese immigrants in the United States who meet by phone at night for worship and fellowship. More than one hundred people call each night to the Church of Grace in Manhattan's Chinatown, where the pastor leads them in hymn singing and Bible study. Most of the callers are originally from the Fuzhou region of the Fujian province in China, one of the Chinese provinces in which Christianity is spreading quickly.

The immigrants are spread out around the United States, working "bone-wearying 12-hour shifts as stir-fry cooks, dishwashers, deliverymen and waiters at Chinese restaurants, buffets and takeout places."[12] Not speaking English, they are isolated and lonely.

Using free night and weekend cell phone hours, for an hour a night they "sing praises to God over the phone and study shengjing—the Bible—together." The far-flung restaurant workers "have come to form a virtual church on Monday through Thursday nights, deriving spiritual sustenance and companionship."

They form a church. "'It's like there's a giant net, connecting people from all different places together,' said Mr. Chen, speaking in Mandarin." He said that the "Bible study offered him a lifeline, a rare chance to escape. 'For us brothers and sisters who are out of state,' he said, 'the Bible study over the phone is central to our lives.'"[13] Sometimes Bible study participants ask questions.

Sometimes they share news about their lives and pray for each other. Though unable to see each other, they form a community as they listen and are heard.

The teacher, speaking about the disciples going from village to village with Jesus, tells the restaurant workers that they "could go from buffet house to buffet house, planting seeds of faith wherever they went." Grace flows to them and through them to the world.

Chosen or unchosen, cultivation of some kind happens. The philosopher William James wrote, "All our life, so far as it has definite form, is but a mass of habits—practical, emotional, intellectual—systematically organized for our weal or woe, and bearing us irresistibly toward our destiny, whatever the latter may be."[14] We may choose garden living.

The hope behind this book is that as you read about a spirituality of cultivation (while immersed in a circus of distractions) you will be formed by God's grace, as I have been formed while I have written it. My own experience is written into the book, and writing the book has been part of God's cultivation of my life.

The following chapters offer some understandings and suggestions for practices that open our hearts and lives to God's cultivation, even in the midst of a circus-like culture. Some of the practices are familiar—like listening and friendship—though often neglected. Some are perhaps less familiar—like sabbath keeping, praying with Scripture and spiritual direction. All the practices can be a means of God's grace, enabling us to reorient ourselves toward God, our deepest selves and others.

For Reflection

1. When speaking to his disciples, Jesus invited them to "consider the lilies." Imagine God inviting you to consider the garden of your life. You may want to draw it. What does that garden com-

municate to you about what you and God are cultivating in your life? Spend time with that image and see if there's a story to it.

2. The culture presses us toward the circus polarities of performing and spectating. How does that environment shape the way you live?

3. Spend time considering what moves you from the garden to the circus, and then reflect on what moves you from the circus to the garden.

The Way of Cultivation

Ground that drinks up the rain falling on it repeatedly,
and that produces a crop useful to those for whom
it is cultivated, receives a blessing from God.

Hebrews 6:7

*A*FEW YEARS AGO ON A WARM FALL DAY, I officiated at a
wedding. Not being an ordained clergyperson, I'd never
before accepted such an invitation, but I was assured it would be
legal if I followed county guidelines. I was honored to participate—also awed and a bit apprehensive.

On the Saturday of the rehearsal, I waited in a small room with
the groom and his friends as we prepared to rehearse the ceremony.
The groomsmen, wearing jeans and polo shirts, were boisterous:
fist-bumping, high-fiving, making work phone calls and also
checking out the scores of college football games.

The next day was the wedding, and we again waited in the same
room behind the altar of the church. The mood had shifted, and a
hush fell over the men, now dressed in black tie and patent leather

shoes. I felt it too. They and I were part of the holy practice of joining two people together before the eyes of God and the community. We were in the splash zone of grace.

As the groom, his groomsmen and I waited for the wedding coordinator to text the best man that it was time for us to walk out to the front of the church and receive the bridal procession, no one surfed the Net or made phone calls. The only phone in sight had the sacred duty of letting us know when to process to the altar. Our attention focused and our hearts engaged, we had left the shallows of the circus and moved to the depths of holiness.

Sitting with the men, I thought about other weddings. My father and husband had sat in similar rooms waiting to go forth and greet their brides, though they weren't waiting for text messages to tell them when to do so. Despite changes in time and technology, all these men were held in the enfolding awe of the occasion.

After the bride and her attendants joined us at the altar, we began the marriage ceremony of the Episcopal Book of Common Prayer. Ancient words signaled transformation: "Dearly beloved: We have come together in the presence of God to witness and bless the joining together of this man and this woman in Holy Matrimony."[1] The couple's vows and our witness were forging a marriage out of two single people, a consecrated union reflecting the spiritual marriage of Christ and the church. The adventure of marriage began.

HOLY MIXED METAPHORS

On that wedding day, two persons were engrafted together and embarked on an adventure. As persons, couples and communities, we are grafted into the Living Vine. We're also adventuring.

As we seek Life, metaphors of rootedness and journeying, so antithetical to the circus imagery of spectating and performing, collaborate. Rootedness and journeying are fundamental to biblical and cultural understandings of life, each capturing an aspect of how we live in the space between our birth and our eventual completion.

Matt, the middle-aged man who felt he was in a rut, spoke about not making progress "on the way forward, the way of growth, even flourishing." In doing so he joined journey imagery about the way forward with garden imagery about flourishing, thus communicating a robustly paradoxical picture of the cultivated life.

When I was a child, English teachers told me not to mix metaphors in my writing. For example, if time is a river in which we swim, scarcely conscious of its movement yet inexorably held in its current, then don't muddy the image with economic concepts about spending, investing, wasting and saving time. "Time is a river" captures part of our experience, while "time is money" expresses another aspect, and writing instructors would have us hold those metaphorical domains apart.

Yet some of humankind's oldest texts were written by people who mixed metaphors wisely in order to express the seemingly contradictory structure of experience through analogy to things tangible and visible. The Hebrew and Christian Scriptures are saturated with these mixed images, and a particularly potent one for the cultivation of our lives is "walking trees."

When Jesus restores sight to the blind man in Mark's Gospel, partway through the healing process the man tells Jesus that he sees people who look like "walking trees" (Mark 8:24). In Greek, they looked like *dendra . . . peripatountas*. Notice the relation to English: they look like peripatetic dendrites. Psalmists, the prophets Isaiah and Jeremiah, and Christ's apostle Paul all seem to have seen the same image, for we repeatedly read that we are walking on the path while we also are rooted and planted. Most notably in Paul's letter to the Colossians, he instructs his readers, as they continue in Christ, to "walk . . . rooted" (2:6-7 ESV), which in the Greek sounds like we're to be peripatetic rhizomes.[2] The word Paul uses for "walk" is often translated into English as "live" by translators to avoid the jarringly mixed metaphor of a tree walking.

Thus, Scripture describes a spirituality of cultivation: We journey *and* are rooted as we live in fullness toward our completion. We are encouraged to "walk, rooted" in the sphere of God's grace as we live each day on earth.

All metaphors and linguistic images are lenses that focus on certain aspects of reality while excluding others. Paul allowed that we will always be growing in our ability to grasp the magnitude of God: "For we know only in part, and we prophesy only in part; but when the complete comes, the partial will come to an end" (1 Corinthians 13:9-10). We see through a glass darkly—at times with great clarity, more often with less. Metaphors help us see more clearly in the murky environment of our humanness.

We walk in faith as we grow more and more rooted in the soil of grace. Both realms of imagery are needed. On the one hand, to see people as on the path but not rooted would overlook the garden's embeddedness in soil and its receptivity to the care of the gardener. Garden imagery draws our attention to variations due to seasons, weather and age, and ultimately the generativity of bearing fruit and enriching the soil. Life in the garden entails the rooted realities of interdependence and intimacy.

On the other hand, to see people as like trees but not walking on a path neglects our forward movement through time and space, the development of our stories and progress toward destiny. The narrative of a journey tells of places seen, left behind and appearing on the horizon.

The melding of the imaginative domains of garden and journey allows for some of the wisdom we see in modern developmental theory, which portrays human psychosocial development as involving growth in autonomy (like the forward movement on the road) coupled with maturing in interdependency (like the ecology of the garden).[3] These forms of growth are experienced and must be accommodated in the human relationships of family, friendship and community, as well as in our relationship with God.

Many of us, like the biblical writers, move easily between these two metaphorical domains without skipping a beat. Recently in spiritual direction a woman said to me, "It's a long slog right now as I try to keep on keeping on in the way God would have me go. But I sense that the journey is beginning to bear fruit."

This woman, like Matt, used the word *way* to convey destiny— how God would have her go as she moves toward what Paul calls "the complete" (1 Corinthians 13:10). Matt experiences regret about his lack of spiritual progress, sharing the woman's desire to be walking on the right path while bearing fruit in the world.

The cultivated life is one of *persevering in our longing*. In the garden and on the trail, grace collaborates with dedication. Our completion comes toward us as we move toward it, and this is all part of what Paul calls the "still more excellent way" (1 Corinthians 12:31).

The word *way* overflows with spiritual salience:

- a manner or mode (for example, a wedding is a way to start a marriage)
- progress on a course (making one's way forward, say, toward "the complete")
- customs (such as the way of the disciples, including spiritual disciplines)
- the condition of thriving (life rooted in a good or "still more excellent" way)
- the ethical or unethical course of life (the right or wrong way, as in the way of righteousness/unrighteousness)

Matt's uses of the word *way* expressed several of these definitions. He was hoping for a way forward, a path, possibly a plan to help him alter the story of his life. Though acknowledging the difficulty of changing his ways, he sought help in finding practices to cultivate good and right living. The woman who was slogging along God's way, the students in my spirituality classes, people in spiritual direction, and I too, like Matt, are looking for the spiritual way of flourishing.

Participating in Our Cultivation

The word *way* also conveys confirmation, referring to rightness and truth. People use the word in casual interchanges about veracity. One person makes a statement, for instance, "I saw a whale," to which the listener, expressing rhetorical doubt and amazement, responds, "No way!" The first person, rebutting the doubter, then exclaims, "Way!" As Matt entertained the hope of changing his ways to live more and more the way God would have him live, I felt confirmation well up in me. For it is "way true" that we can change our spiritual ways. I've witnessed it far more often than I've seen a whale.

The "still more excellent way" involves living in God's grace while "walking, rooted." Such a life doesn't just happen. Cultivation is required.

Most people who embrace some kind of spirituality believe we can continue to grow and learn our whole life long. A nurse who cares for people as they approach death writes that they "grow a lot when they are faced with their own mortality." She observes that each person she has cared for "experienced a variety of emotions, as expected, denial, fear, anger, remorse, more denial and eventually acceptance. Every single patient found their peace before they departed though, every one of them."[4]

Christians through the centuries have expressed conviction about following the way of cultivation throughout the life course. John Calvin wrote that "the life of believers, longing constantly for their appointed status, is like adolescence."[5] It isn't a stage we outgrow in this life. In our spiritual life we are always like adolescents, the Latin word for adolescent meaning "to become adult" and incorporating the understanding that we grow through being nourished. Calvin's statement is not a diagnosis of immaturity but an affirmation of the completion we're moving toward with hope, and a recognition that thriving is dependent on being fed and cared for, not just mustering our willpower.

In 1 Corinthians 13:10, Paul's word for "the complete" is *telos*, often translated as "perfection" and thus creating a host of difficulties through the ages for people who readily assume the lonely post of dutiful perfectionism. Spiritual completion is not a matter of willfully straining after an ideal. It is, rather, a relational fullness of life that is forever unfolding and developing, like the way tree trunks thicken as sun, water and nutrients are imbibed. In our living, we aren't supposed to come to the end of our growing, or even of heartfelt yearning for it. Nor are we to become independent pursuers of growth.

The "complete comes." It isn't wholly dependent on or achieved by our striving toward it. The "complete" that comes is God, and "God is love" (1 John 4:16). God's "seed abides" (1 John 3:9) and germinates in us. The Giver of Life participates with us in our living.

A letter by Karl Barth, the influential Protestant theologian of the last century, captures this sense of participating in our cultivation. Asked near the end of his life if he would write an article reflecting on the future of theology and what tasks and problems he would set for himself if he were to start his academic career afresh, Barth declined, responding that he had no plans for the future. In fact, he felt his own life had come to him, more than being planned and built by him.

Though famous for his extensive—seemingly planned—volumes of systematic theology, Barth wrote about his books, lectures and sermons that they were like trees "of all kinds, big and little, that sprang up, grew and spread before me." They were given to him:

> Their existence did not depend on me; rather I had to watch over their development with all my attention. Or I might say that I feel like a man in a boat that I must row and steer diligently; but it swims in a stream I do not control. It glides along between ever new and often totally strange shores, carrying me toward the goals set for me, goals that I see and choose only when I approach them.[6]

Barth experienced himself as participating in the cultivation of his life. Trees were given to him to tend, and so was a stream for him to navigate. He was, as it were, a walking (or rowing) tree—bearing the fruit engendered in him and nearing his good completion as it came toward him.

PRACTICES FORM US

Near the end of his magisterial *Four Quartets*, T. S. Eliot addressed how we live in the garden. There we experience a shaft of sunlight, the scent of wild thyme, a waterfall. He wrote that these encounters provide hints and guesses, while the greater part of our living is "prayer, observance, discipline, thought and action."[7] These are ways our lives are cultivated—through ordinary daily practices and by solemn, rare-in-a-lifetime practices, like weddings.

Matt specifically wanted to know about practices that would help him stay on the right path, bear spiritual fruit in the world and have some hope of ending well. Like Karl Barth, Matt believes life is given to him, and he hopes to "row and steer diligently" as he lives it.

Ways of growing in the form of spiritual practices have always been fundamental to personal faith and to the life of faith communities, Christian and otherwise. More and more, however, long-time Christians lament that their churches and communities—and they themselves—have lost touch with those ways. "Deeds, more than creeds," some cry, longing for a corrective reordering of priorities.

The word *religion* comes to us from the Latin *religiare*, meaning to bind together as ligaments bind muscle to bone in our bodies. As the sun sets on Friday evening and Jewish believers' hearts open to the arrival of God's holy day, they experience themselves as bound to God and to other Jews around the world and throughout history. Religions, through beliefs and practices, bind us to deities, meanings and communities, all of these elements composing tradition, a way of spiritual cultivation.

The book of Psalms, the Bible's prayer book, begins with a poem about the way of cultivation. The first word of Psalm 1 is *ashrei*, often translated as "blessed" or "happy." Like many Hebrew words, it also has a concrete meaning that derives from its relation to the Hebrew verb *asher*, which means "being on the road" or "going straight" on the path.[8] Judaism throughout the millennia has cultivated practices of worship and right living that help people walk rightly and be happy.

While walking, the psalmist tells us, the blessed person is like a tree planted by streams of water whose leaves never wither and that bears fruit in season—in short, a walking tree.[9] This is cultivation, for the Lord watches over the way of the righteous and is responsible for the life-giving water (Psalm 1:6). The walking tree is nourished.

Centuries later Jesus drew on way imagery. Shortly before his death he spoke to his disciples and, responding to a question from the doubting disciple Thomas, said, "I am the way, the truth, and the life" (John 14:6). As comprehensive as dictionary definitions of *way* are, Jesus adds a new one: the way is not only a path and a state of fulfillment but the particular person of Jesus, God with us, then and now.

Early in the fifth century, the Roman African priest Augustine of Hippo succinctly captured the multiplicity of "the way" in a Christmas sermon. He told his listeners, "Be in attendance at the manger; do not be ashamed of being the Lord's donkey. You will be carrying Christ; you will not go astray walking along the way because the Way is sitting on you."[10] Augustine is sandwiched in grace—on the way, carrying the Way, and no doubt directed by the Way as well. Karl Barth imagines that he sits in a boat on the stream of God, which carries him toward the goals set for him. Jesus tells us we are branches in the fruit-generating vine that he is (John 15:5). We, too, sandwiched in grace, are a nourished, ever-growing conduit between the vine and the fruit.

THE WAY OF LIFE

The way as a caring, guiding Person holds primacy. This is the most significant ligament that binds people in Christian faith. From that follows the way as posture, practice, destination and understanding, but the relationship between God and believer is what undergirds all belief and practice.

Religion is anathema to many people in North America, and the terms *spirituality* and *way of life* seem to be acceptable substitutes, as in the frequently heard North American assertion that Buddhism is a way of life, not a religion. Some Asian religions, often in secularized forms, appeal to people in parts of the world where Christianity has ossified into systematized doctrines, behavioral codes and stale or staged worship experiences. Spiritually seeking people are understandably attracted to a way of life that emphasizes meaning and practices more than propositions of belief.

For many Westerners raised in traditional Judeo-Christian cultures, religion has become depleted, no longer a full-bodied, life-integrating, practical and moral philosophy, such as that suggested by the welcome words *way of life*. It is through lived faith that vitality is breathed into religion, and we have lost touch with the practices of spiritual cultivation that can bind a faithful person to God and people.

Harvey Cox has claimed that *spirituality* is a better word to use today than *religion* because it describes "a way of life rather than a doctrinal structure."[11] Moreover, he advocated retiring the term *Christianity* and retrieving *the Way,* the earliest Christian name for the community of Jesus' followers.[12] Peruvian theologian Gustavo Gutiérrez wrote that the way, described in Acts, "reflects at once a manner of thinking and a manner of acting—in short, a way of life; nothing falls outside this way."[13] It involves thought and action, rooted and grounded in the God who is love. Staying connected to the One in whom we abide is the challenge of Christian spirituality.

The millions of people eagerly purchasing spirituality books (including more than a thousand written since 2000 on the subject of happiness) may be seeking an answer to Eliot's question, "Where is the Life we have lost in living?"[14] How can we rediscover and cultivate the way we have lost? Eliot considered this as a matter of life and death.

Most of us who live in the notably individualistic cultures of North America and Western Europe do not express our faith in public very often. We neither pray on our streets at set hours of the day, as is done in Muslim countries, nor devotionally prostrate ourselves repeatedly while slowly ambulating clockwise, as in Buddhist cultures. I can't think of a religious season recognized by restaurants throughout a Western country in the way that present-day Russian restaurants offer Lenten menus for Christians who are fasting. However, when moved, shaken and unsettled to the depths of our being by events that touch us as a people rather than just as individuals, even we who live in secular countries gather together, light candles and sing. Doing so is a shared spiritual practice elicited by extraordinary events.

Aside from extraordinary events (like national disasters) and ceremonies (such as weddings) that draw us together, how do we engage in ordinary daily practices that enable us to open our heart and cultivate our soul? It is these spiritual practices, in particular, that vitalize our ties to God's Spirit and to community.

NARRATIVES ILLUMINATE: AN ILLUSTRATION

Words and images shape the way we experience and think, beliefs and practices form us as individuals and communities, and narratives illuminate truths about human life. Stories help us know who we are and what we're to do. The word *narrative* derives from ancient words for knowledge, and narratives teach us about what's real, what's possible and what makes sense. Stories shed light on our way.

At the end of Luke's Gospel (24:13-35) we read about two people who meet the resurrected Jesus on the road to Emmaus. They're grieving the persecution destroying their community, most significantly the execution of their teacher and friend, unrecognized as the person speaking to them while they walk along. Some New Testament scholars claim these people are Cleopas (appearing with a similar name in John 10:25) and his wife, Mary, Jesus' aunt who had stood at the foot of the cross witnessing the death of her nephew, the one she believed to be God's Son. Days later, having observed the

Jewish sabbath with their family in Jerusalem, the couple fled the city.

On the seven-mile walk to Emmaus, Jesus approached them. We can imagine that this is the same person Paul calls "the complete," coming to them from the far side of a completed human life. Without fanfare or "ta-dah!" triumphalism, he arrived unobtrusively so they weren't frightened into silence or flight. He expressed interest in them: "What are you discussing with each other while you walk along?" (Luke 24:17). His question brought them to a standstill. In their stopping, their deeper feelings arose.

What we then read are the words of traumatized people. Hopes and fears mingle. Confusion reigns. They had hoped Jesus was the Messiah, but he was killed. Angels at the empty tomb told some women that Jesus had risen from the dead, but no one had seen him. Yes . . . but.

The stories they were telling themselves about Jesus' death affected what they could see and comprehend as he stood before them. After drawing out their story, Jesus told them the narrative of his life, foretold in Scripture and lived in their lifetime. Yet they still did not recognize Jesus.

Jesus talked with them as they walked the road with him, and their own story grew as new experience informed understanding. Eventually, after arriving at their home in Emmaus, they recognized Jesus at the table in the breaking of the bread. In that moment light was shed on their past experiences in Jerusalem, and they remembered that their hearts had burned within them as Jesus spoke with them on the road.

With their sudden recognition, Jesus disappeared. Without his accompaniment and seemingly without fear, they then hurried back to their community in Jerusalem with joyful news. History was not rewritten (they still were bereft), but it was illuminated by the ongoing story of grace.

RECOGNIZING AND CHOOSING CULTIVATION

The stories of our lives hold the possibility of illumination, by God's grace. We catch glimpses of the Holy in our lives and in the lives of others. This nurtures hope. The narratives in this book are ones that shed light on the cultivated life in a variety of people's experiences. They give us models to ponder, even as they raise questions about our own lives. They have helped me see what cultivated lives can look like.

Some of the stories told in this book are private ones, drawn from my daily life and also from people I've encountered far from my home, that have taught me something about the focal practice of the chapter. Other stories in this book are public ones—from Scripture, newspapers and books—that show how the practice addressed in the chapter has global resonance and can transform the world. Immigrants, a hostage and other people introduced in the chapters ahead have maintained beliefs and practices of faith that sustained them in exceptionally difficult situations. Their faithfulness lights our own way of spiritual cultivation.

Directing attention to the cultivation of our lives, chapters elucidating concepts will be followed by practical chapters concerning what we may do—through prayer, observance, discipline, thought and action—to cultivate our lives. Even in the context of an increasingly circus-like society and with our own imperfect vision so reliant on hints and guesses, we can participate in our growing. Discipline joins desire as we turn and return to God.

The time-tested and cherished disciplines of the Christian tradition, many having Jewish roots, require opening our hearts and minds in love. In that sense they are contemplative, for another person or Person is the object of our receptive attention. Such practices are often eclipsed by louder demands in most of our lives, and many of the practices receive scant attention even in the literatures of spirituality. They are, on the whole, private practices that we can cultivate and that, in turn, will facilitate our cultivation.

The spiritual practices are portable and flexible, and hermit vows are not required. People in all times and places, in exile and enslavement, cities and the countryside, have engaged in these practices. They do not require the presence of worshiping communities but are wholly compatible with and benefit from congregational life. They do require listening, and listening requires openness. Difficult as the movements of receiving and listening are, Scripture shows us it is possible to shift into those postures, as the couple did on the Emmaus road.

FOR REFLECTION

1. Scripture depicts human beings as "walking trees." Consider how you are on the right path. What does that image feel like? What aspects of your life do you associate with that metaphor of right living?

2. Then consider how you are rooted and grounded. What does that image feel like? What aspects of your life do you associate with that metaphor of right living?

3. Remember a time when the story you were telling yourself about your life was radically changed by an encounter with God or some manifestation of grace, as happened to the people at the table in Emmaus. Tell that story. Write it, or share it with someone.

FINDING AND RECEIVING REFRESHMENT

The Spirit of the Lord GOD is upon Me,
Because the LORD has anointed Me
To preach good tidings to the poor; . . .
To give them beauty for ashes,
The oil of joy for mourning,
The garment of praise for the spirit of heaviness;
That they may be called trees of righteousness.

ISAIAH 61:1, 3 NKJV

PRACTICES ARE CRUCIAL TO HOW WE SEEK GOD, yet we are often oblivious to our spiritual practices. Our receptivity to God's refreshing grace is cultivated through practices that help us open to God and our deepest selves; therefore, in spirituality courses I often ask people to listen to their lives, noticing over the course of a week what they do routinely that turns their hearts toward God.

In the second week of a class I was teaching, a man reported that he had done a "spiritual cardiac assessment" and discovered that showering is what turns his heart toward God. As he showers, he explained to us, he can't work and cannot be interrupted. He prays. In the shower this overworked lawyer relaxes and experiences peace, remembering that God loves him. The overwhelming concerns of his daily life diminish in the light of that cosmic perspective. His soul receives refreshment. "And," he said, "during especially stressful times, I may take two showers a day!"

SPIRITUAL REFRESHMENT

My student had never before realized that showering was part of how he is cultivated by God and wouldn't have listed it as a spiritual practice or cited it as a part of his religion. Living in a culture disinclined to acknowledge the formative power of practice, he had never thought about his personal spiritual practices. In fact, many Christians have little awareness of what our spiritual practices are, though most of us find ways of receiving refreshment for our souls.

In 1992 the American Academy of Religion recognized Christian spirituality as an academic field of inquiry, a legitimate discipline having to do with the understanding and practice of religion. Its scope includes beliefs and practices that connect us to God, who has been revealed through Jesus Christ and continues to be present with us in the Holy Spirit. It examines not only what we believe but also how we know God, given that God's love and truth are communicated to us through a variety of means, including Scripture, community, persons, history, experience and our own efforts to know God and live as we are called to live. All this is the stuff of spirituality.

The time-pressured lawyer came to a better understanding of God, himself and his life through his discipline of showering. It shaped how he went about his day, just as saying the Jesus Prayer or having a morning quiet time aerates days that can be spiritually suffocating.

The discipline of Christian spirituality is not wholly objective; rather, it is said to be "self-implicating."[1] This means that who we are informs our understanding of God, faith and discipleship. Conversely, what we discover about God, faith and discipleship affects who we are and how we live. Spirituality differs from some other fields of inquiry in this respect. Many academic and scientific fields have become increasingly aware of how the person of the observer affects the phenomena being observed. But even so, astronomy is less self-implicating than spirituality. The physicist's personal story does not profoundly shape what is seen through the telescope. Nor does what is seen there necessarily have an impact on the physicist's comportment in daily life.

But in our spiritual lives, we are branches in the very vine we are contemplating. What we discover there shapes us profoundly in both our understanding and our way of life. The lawyer trusts that God is present in the sanctuary of his shower and that God welcomes and loves him just as he is. Those beliefs inform his action and experience. In turn, as the water pours over his stress-pummeled body, the peace and love he receives through prayer inform his understanding of God.

Our attention to spirituality affects our lives and therefore is always about spiritual formation. The lawyer said, "Since I recognized what I was doing, I've been showering preemptively—before particularly difficult meetings. I'm reminded of God's grace by the dampness of my hair!" A key way of experiencing Life in our lives is attending to those lives—watching them, listening to them and noticing the signs of God's life in them.

The couple on the Emmaus road brought their story of recent trauma and dashed hopes to bear on their encounter with Jesus.

Their experiences shaped what they were able to see and grasp. Their time with Jesus on the road and at the table in Emmaus then altered what they knew to be true. Their vision was refreshed, and they shared it with others. When we engage in spiritual practices, we too can expect to be changed and, by grace, refreshed.

BRANCHES IN THE VINE

Any book about life is also about death, and that's true of this one in terms of both subject matter—how to live a cultivated life while moving toward a graced completion—and also my personal experience during the time I was writing. *The Cultivated Life* was quickening in my imagination as I accompanied my mother and father to the completion of their long lives in the summer of 2012, my father dying just three months after my mother, quite literally of a broken heart as the biochemistry of grief surged through his heart that had loved my mother for sixty years. Writing the book has been self-implicating: my own spiritual experience is woven into it, and writing it has been a part of God's cultivation of my life.

Being with my parents in their final days granted me an unobstructed view of ordinary "cultivated" lives. I listened and watched. It seemed to me that my parents did not lose Life in living, even as their bodies deteriorated and they readied themselves to leave us. What Mom and Dad showed me in their living and dying suffuses this book and would have done so even if I had chosen not to mention them. Inspired by Belden C. Lane, who wrote of his mother's death in his elegant, wise book about wilderness spirituality, *The Solace of Fierce Landscapes: Exploring Desert and Mountain Spirituality*,[2] I have incorporated my parents in this book about a cultivation spirituality.

Not surprisingly given the midlife season I'm in, other people I have loved and listened to have recently come to the ends of their lives. One of these people is Peter Ogle. Shortly after the first Easter without my parents, I received a message from a friend telling me that Peter, an acquaintance of mine from many years ago, was dying of cancer and had just been told he had about a hundred days left to live. He had begun a blog following his 2006 diagnosis of melanoma, and I immediately went to the site.[3]

What struck me was Peter's faithful living even while walking in the valley of the shadow of death. In the fifth century Benedict of Nursia instructed monks to ponder death every day as a spiritual discipline informing and shaping their lives, and as I read Peter's blog I realized that was exactly what he'd been doing since his diagnosis.

I wrote to Peter and expressed my sadness about his illness. I also told him about the book I was writing and that it seemed to me he'd been living a "cultivated life." He wrote back, "The Cultivated Life? I strive for it, fail mostly, but find great joy in the effort."[4] Those words of his, written just a few weeks before his death, have shed light on my writing.

Even as he lay dying, Peter continued to strive joyfully in life—a saintly mingling of the solemn practice of *memento mori* (remembering death) with the zesty practice of *carpe diem* (seize or pluck the ripeness of the day).[5] He sought life in the present moment as he prepared for the next life, guided by the Way as he walked the remaining steps of his way. Despite the failures he perceived and the tragedy of dying too young, Peter wrote that he was finding "great joy in the effort" to live a cultivated life.

Listening to my parents and Peter as they lived their final days has taught me how to better live my own ordinary days. Peter was a writer who chose to share his inner life with others, so I was able to read his reflections. My parents were private people, and I learned about the cultivation of their lives by observing them over the decades we shared.

GOLDEN DAYS AHEAD

My father and Peter both had gardens. They understood how sunlight, soil, water and human care join forces to nurture life, which emerges as new shoots, strong roots, blossoms, fruit and canopy. Shortly before his death Peter wrote,

> It helps to have had many warm, sunny days in which we have all gotten out into the garden, to do some cleanup and spring prep. I never guessed we'd get the garden whipped into shape this spring, but thanks to my willing minions [mostly family], we've done it. The azaleas are blooming, and the berries fattening up in anticipation of more golden days ahead. We can smell the lilac already. . . . Life is hard, but life is good. We are all blessed to be a part of God's great creation.[6]

Peter was keenly aware of "God's great creation" enveloping and supporting the living and the dying. He died two weeks after that post, a few months short of his sixtieth birthday. The berries and lilacs he tended—and in a holy, mysterious way Peter himself—continued on into the golden days he imagined.

In the summer of my parents' deaths, I too sought comfort from gardens, actual and literary. My parents' final years were spent mostly in a sunroom that opened onto my father's garden. Outside and near the door between my father's sofa and my mother's chair stands a mature lemon tree. On warm days when the door is open, its scent still freshens the rooms of the house. I live miles away, and the family members presently living in the home don't share my father's enthusiasm for growing things, so the garden is wilder now. The roses are leggy, and lemons weigh down the limber branches that imprudently produce such overabundance. My father's cultivating care would have relieved the burdened branches and given the rosebushes the severe tonic of a late-winter haircut. But overgrown or trimmed, the fragrance remains.

In my grief I was also drawn to children's books in which bereft children sought grace and hope in gardens. Those gardens went through untended seasons, as did the children. The orphaned children encountered people or animals that moved their hearts, but it was green things that most profoundly communicated deep hope to them. In a secret garden it was discovered that even after a tragic death, life continued. Some degree of human cultivation was required, but the force of life throbbed upward from roots to canopy, bringing forth blossoms and seed, providing shelter and nurture to those who received it, including birds, animals and grieving children. Gardens are able to hold death and life.

In Elizabeth Goudge's *The Little White Horse,* thirteen-year-old Maria, whose parents have died, goes through a hidden doorway in a wall and finds not only beautiful greenery but also a "stream bubbling up out of the ground, forcing its way through a choking mass of fallen dead beech leaves," and then flowing downhill to the village.[7] The experience moves the girl to kneel and pray. Her soul is refreshed as the garden extends God's grace to her.

My parents' deaths were good and in no way tragic, but, like the fictional children, I am bereft of their presence in my life. Stories of children's souls being rehydrated in gardens have brought me solace, as has the beauty of the earth. Sunlight slanting through trees seems to break through to the core of what matters. Breezes carrying the scent of fruit and flower bring comfort. Peter Ogle's final writings show how even as life ebbed, he found grace in a garden that he tended alongside those he loved.

The deaths of these good people taught me about how the garden of God's grace is present even in the most difficult of circumstances, and that flourishing is possible as death approaches. The heroics around life extension can become circuslike as we jump at every medical procedure, however futile. At the passive end of the circus polarities, too, we can numb ourselves to the realities of death, thus losing connection with those we love even before death arrives.

CONCEIVING OF GRACE

My parents and Peter Ogle lived in close proximity to actual gardens. They also participated in the cultivation of their lives and those of other people, inviting others to join them as they lived to the end of their days. They were walking trees: walking with God and all the while becoming increasingly rooted and planted in grace. Their gardens held death, growth and the hope of "golden days ahead," even as the Complete came to them. Grace flowed to and through them.

Fewer and fewer of us live close to the land. Many of us have only minimal acquaintance with trees. The media by which we are so forcefully cultivated offer metaphors of human existence that contrast with the organic rhythms of garden living. Conflict rises ("tensions are escalating in the Middle East") and financial markets fall ("the Dow tumbled today"). We receive bulletins about the "War on Terror" and "fight" diseases of various kinds. Life is often spoken of in competitive imagery as we advance, make our moves and, we hope, win. Death, if mentioned, is often viewed as an enemy to be defeated.

How we act is affected by how we conceive of things in our minds, even when the conceptualization is unconscious. Moreover, our spiritual experience—so elusive and often beyond language— is received, metabolized and communicated through language, which bridges the conscious and unconscious. Scripture is rich in familiar metaphors that reverberate in the depths of our souls, and its "sacred texts are chronicles of experience, armouries of metaphor, and purveyors of an interpretive tradition."[8] Experience of God's commonwealth as a garden in which we are cultivated is a sustaining resource in a circuslike culture.

In my work as a spiritual director I witness how metaphors collaborate in a person's life, some representing the life the person experiences when oriented toward God, and some showing how life is experienced when God is forgotten. An aspect of the art of spiritual direction is tuning in to those metaphors and inviting the directee to explore them. A spiritual listening practice explicitly encourages the speaker to "choose life," and metaphors can help people do just that.

RECEIVING REFRESHMENT:
AN ILLUSTRATION FROM SPIRITUAL DIRECTION

Laura came to see me for spiritual direction late one afternoon and spent the first part of our hour talking about the pressures of working, mothering young children and commuting. She felt as though her life couldn't fit into a day. She used circuslike phrases: "I'm running as fast as I can," "I'm squeezed dry" and "I've maxed out every moment I have, multitasking and pounding." This is her reality. She enjoys her work and loves her children, but there's not enough time to do all she wants to do.

After listening, I wondered aloud what experience she had of spiritual things in days and nights so squeezed and stuffed. That was when this vivacious extrovert said, "When I'm most in tune with the Holy, I feel like a sponge." In full workday makeup, high heels and hair tinted magenta, Laura looked nothing like a sponge. But she lit up as she said the word.

Focusing on the image that so clearly appealed to her, I said, "A sponge? Tell me about that." Laura told me that she gets caught up in the conflicting demands of work and family and feels "scattered," "frenetic" and "hyper." When she has time to be quiet in the virtual solitude of the crowded subway on the way to work, however, she feels "grace" oozing into her. It's as though a well is filling up from the bottom, the water slowly rising, filling the pores of her soul. She said she's like a sponge in a container, snug and at peace, as the water fills her.

I said, "So the water—the grace—permeates you cell by cell?"

"Yes, that's it. It's not that it washes over me, or that I float in it. It is in me, cell by cell. I'm penetrated, changed . . . and also held." I asked about the feelings associated with this, and she responded, "It's peaceful. Deeply peaceful." Laura breathed in deeply, as though demonstrating the peace. I could feel it too. "There's nothing I have to do. I just rest in it. I'm nourished."

I explored the parameters of the peace in time: Did it linger after she arrived at her subway station?

"It does linger," she answered. "As I walk the final blocks to work, I move more slowly, more aware of my feet on the pavement, the air on my face, what I'm seeing. There's no anxiety. No mental chatter about the various things I have to do."

When that happens she is keenly aware of the present moment and her physical experience. She said, "My body feels whole. All of me feels whole, filled, held. That's how I feel when I'm at work on those days. I can hear and take note of the tasks and the colleagues without being reactive. I have a kind of breadth, weight, gravity, buoyancy—something like that—that gives me peace even in the rush of work." Laura took another deep breath and enacted a floating movement with her arms.

This metaphor shows grace at work. Laura receives it, it changes her, and then it flows through her into her interactions with others. The structure of grace is flow.

When Laura has received the "water," she enters into a different existential state, even though still in her everyday circumstances. The image fosters resiliency. As she listened to her life and told me about the remembered experience, she reexperienced grace—communion with the Holy.

Laura spoke of feeling like a sponge being filled with the water of grace—calm, peaceful, contented. Metaphors link our thoughts and our bodies, and she enacted her peaceful state by extending her arms as though she were a floating sponge. She was receptive, and her receptivity was amplified as she explored the image in my presence. I received grace, too, as I listened.

Laura's experience in prayer is akin to that of being a well-watered garden, and as I sat with this grace-saturated woman, Isaiah's words came to mind:

> The LORD will guide you continually,
>> and satisfy your needs in parched places,
>> and make your bones strong;
> and you shall be like a watered garden,
>> like a spring of water,
>> whose waters never fail. (Isaiah 58:11)

I pictured the sponginess of my lawn after a heavy rain, water spurting up with each step I take. So it is with Laura: in the midst of public transportation and rush-hour congestion, she becomes like a watered garden as she opens her heart in prayer.

THE SOUL'S CULTIVATION

Scripture offers a spirituality of cultivation, and the concept of cultivating souls finds biblical grounding in the words of the prophets and psalmists. In the garden of the Vinegrower, the One into whom we are engrafted tells us that each "branch that bears fruit he prunes to make it bear more fruit" (John 15:2). Picture the branch engrafted in the vine. Prayer connects us with that vine, allowing inner stillness and an open orientation to God through which flows the refreshment of grace. Tended by the Vinegrower, we grow in life and fruition. These images Jesus used come to us today in our urban, industrialized environments, so far from vineyards. They assure us that even in congested, noisy places like subways, we are being cultivated. Even in shower stalls. Even in the shadow of death.

The earliest definitions of *cultivation* do not include human cultivation or address urban environments. They are purely agricultural, concerning tilling, planting, growing and pruning. The concept broadened in the seventeenth century and later to include the tending of knowledge and social refinement, such that we might think of Jane Austen's Mr. Darcy as a cultivated gentleman of the early nineteenth century. In the twentieth century the word expanded even more to include the cultivation of minds and lives through broadcast media. Beyond human and cultural influence, Christian spirituality situates the cultivation of our souls within our relationship with God.

In spiritual direction sessions I hear people who seldom put their hands in dirt draw on the whole metaphorical language of cultivation: they speak of how seeds of hope are stirring in the fallow soil of their souls and how God is gently pruning their lives, allowing new shoots to emerge.

In seminary classes I invite students to "draw the tree that you are," and remarkable arbor-spiritualities emerge in their images. Students introduce the class to their drawn selves: a limb that was severed by a lightning-like event, an encircling grove and a nearby stream, a solitary tree in an oasis. Often some fruit is visible in the stretching branches, and occasionally a bird's nest or child's swing. A few times people have introduced the bonsai tree that they are.

For one person it represented cruel pruning, confinement and thwarted growth. For another person the bonsai represented a story of God's focused and intimately attentive care. Images communicate, and the accompanying stories explore and augment them.

As the students introduce the trees that they are to the others in the class, grace flows through the pictures and the stories. We bear witness to spiritual formation. Stories of cultivation, like those of the showering lawyer, Peter Ogle, my parents, and Laura, so markedly different from the competitive ones that dominate our media, hydrate our souls. As we listen, we receive God's grace.

FOR REFLECTION

1. All of us engage in certain behaviors regularly. Over the course of a week, listen to your life, paying particular attention to your habits. Jot down a few notes about them.

2. Which of your habits are helpful? Perhaps they help you pray, relax, trust, speak your truth or extend kindness. Note when it is that you engage in these particular practices. Consider whether you might think of them as spiritual disciplines, practices that help you turn toward God.

3. Select one of the practices you've identified as a spiritual discipline and try it when you are experiencing distress. What do you notice? Does the practice help you receive refreshment?

LISTENING AS A WAY OF RECEIVING CULTIVATION

O you who dwell in the gardens,
my companions are listening for your voice;
let me hear it.

SONG OF SOLOMON 8:13

JUDAISM, CHRISTIANITY AND ISLAM—the Abrahamic faiths—tell a story of how humanity began in a garden and was meant to dwell there. One of the chief concepts embedded in that narrative is that what we take in through our mouths (for instance, forbidden fruit) and our ears (preferably God's Word) matters. We're free to make choices, for good and ill, about what we ingest. But we're asked to listen to the One who spoke creation into being and who still speaks to us about what we ought to take into ourselves. Through listening, relationship is cultivated and refreshment received.

LISTENING TOGETHER

Sometimes graced listening takes place directly through solitary prayer with God, and sometimes it is shared with people. At New College Berkeley we offer group spiritual direction throughout the academic year. In each group four people meet monthly for two hours at a time with a spiritual director who helps them notice God's grace in their lives and also in the lives of the other participants. Once a month I have the joy of listening to the directors reflect on the experience as they come together for supervision.

One October day about halfway through a supervisory meeting, the blessing of the work moved us all to silence. We were listening for God. After a while one director said about the persons in her group, "Their faith affects my faith."

Another said, "God's grace finds the people where they are. They notice it as they listen."

Over the years in the spiritual direction groups we have encountered all of life's joys—childbirths, marriages, graduations, accomplishments, and the discovery and deepening of faith. We've also witnessed the full range of life's hardships, many of them remembered and some of them currently being undergone, including illness, bereavement, disappointment, cruelty, unrealized hopes and doubt. One group accompanied a member as cancer brought life to an end. Together and in all kinds of seasons, people dip into the well of holy grace.

A participant in one of the groups wrote of how God is experienced in the gathering: "Our meeting was alight with God's Spirit, which seemed to be working powerfully to bring peace, strength, clarity, direction, and reverence. . . . Someone brought up Psalm 29, and we closed by reading it. Wow, I must've seen that psalm before, but I feel like it appeared in my Bible just tonight." God's voice is powerful and full of majesty, the psalm says, and that powerful voice was clearly made more audible by the presence of others also listening for God.

ENGAGED ATTENTION: LISTENING AND BEHOLDING

The presence of a spiritual companion or community can help us hear God better and also hear and see ourselves afresh. In many institutional settings this engaged attention is what people long for and don't receive. Even when a person is dying, being seen and heard matters, hallowing life as it ebbs. Hospice volunteers often simply sit with the person who is dying, their listening bringing comfort and reverence.

Engaged attention is different from the focused attention of an accountant scrutinizing a page of numbers for the sake of the mind's comprehension, detached from the knowledge of body and heart. It's also different from the unfocused, fragmented attention of media surfing. Engaged attention requires an openness to the other that involves one's whole self, and this is the stance of contemplation.

Simone Weil wrote that attention "taken to its highest degree, is the same thing as prayer. It presupposes faith and love."[1] The person who is paying attention is trustingly open to the Spirit, which is risky. Those who cultivate gardens lean in too, attending with all their senses to the plants under their care: what is noticed on the surface of a leaf in hue, curl or suppleness; what heard rustling in the canopy of a tree; what smelled, touched or tasted that informs the art of the gardener.

Karl Rahner claimed that when a person "is with God in awe and love, then he is praying."[2] Prayer is more than what we human beings have to say when we close our eyes and bow our heads. In fact, given the participants in the conversation, why would we assume that our words are the ones of greater importance? In prayer we listen for God.

Garden living cultivates in us an open heart, and listening with care is one of its essential practices. Though a core practice of engaged attention, spiritual and otherwise, listening is sorely neglected within our circuslike culture. Just think of an actual circus: Is listening required? The circus was always a great place for us to go as a family with our son Andrew, who's deaf and uses American Sign Language. Not much interpreting needed. At the circus the sound is background to the spectacle.

In our daily lives many of us go about surrounded by sound that envelops us but requires no intentional listening. People say they keep their television sets on "for company," and those sets continue to sound whether anyone's in the room or not. People drive while listening to car radios, scarcely aware of the street noises, but—thankfully—not fully focused on the radio program's content either.

Some environments in our culture intentionally thwart human relating, and many workplaces offer little space for reflection, relationship and refreshment (despite studies showing that our effectiveness and decision-making abilities are depleted by constant labor).[3] People tell me about corporate environments in which they perform their duties for long hours every day. A midlevel manager in a transnational corporation said that there's a code of silence in his open-plan workplace. Whenever he wants to chat with a coworker, he stands up, makes a show of grabbing his empty coffee mug and then walks slowly to the shared kitchen. His friend, noticing, follows. The kitchen becomes a garden space where they breathe more deeply and are refreshed by conversation—and coffee.

Really listening is countercultural and may be becoming increasingly so. In 2007 texting outpaced phone calls for cell phone users.[4] Texting is more efficient, and people seem to prefer the buffered convenience of texting to the more vulnerable experience of speaking with a person who is listening in real time. A disengaged spectator can still text.

Listening and its visual form, beholding, maintain the life-giving connections we need in order to flourish. "Beauty is in the eye of the beholder," the old saying goes. How miserable to lose the experience of beauty by failing to behold, to lose aesthetics by succumbing to that which anesthetizes. And, worse, consider how chilling it is to receive attention that is detached and instrumental—a counterfeit of care—from another person.

The philosopher Charles Taylor wrote, "Nonrecognition or misrecognition can inflict harm, can be a form of oppression, imprisoning someone in a false, distorted, and reduced mode of being."[5] For decades scholars have written critically of the gaze that objectifies for manipulative ends,[6] a gaze employed by institutions, too, to depersonalize people for the sake of control and homogenized identity,[7] like Jean Valjean, the prisoner in *Les Miserables,* seen only as "24601." Without manipulative intent, we too can slip into a detached spectator's gaze, flattening, categorizing and dismissing other people as we fail to listen and behold.

On the day my father died I was struck by the varieties of gazing. I encountered hospital workers to whom my father was a stranger, an old, mortally ill man. They did their jobs well, but they saw Dad's condition more than his person, in part in consideration of patients' privacy. I also saw on the whiteboard facing my father's bed a note written that day by my cousin: "I love you, Uncle Lloyd. Colin." My sleeping father had been beheld with love as he died. Beholding matters.

Our spiritual lives run the risk of becoming devoid of true beholding and listening. If we do not listen to God, the Holy One increasingly becomes a figment of our projections and theology, a safer figure in our lives, perhaps, but a constructed one.

Listening and beholding are ways of paying attention that are participatory acts of empathic connection. They acknowledge more than one perspective and complex of reactions. The listener receives the other, choosing to absorb what the other is communicating. In acts of engaged attention both persons are vulnerable to the other's impression and response. In being beheld and in beholding another visually—"drinking in" the other with one's eyes—we are changed.

BEING LISTENED TO AND LISTENING TO ANOTHER

In the Contemplative Listening course that I've taught for more than a decade to graduate-level theological students, the students write two reflection papers. In the first one they write about a time they were listened to, and in the second about a time they listened to another person. Every year a few students have a hard time remembering someone's listening to them. Their dominant memory is of not having been listened to, and the assignment stirs up disappointed hopes. I encourage them to look back for even a brief experience of being fully heard.

When they do remember a story of being listened to—and they all do eventually remember one—something about the quality of the listening touched their hearts, lingers in memory and moves them again in the remembering. The stories are often about a simple conversation that made a difference. A camp counselor sat with a homesick child and listened while the boy talked about missing his parents and his dog. A teacher stayed after school and listened to a child who had heard her parents argue loudly the night before. A college roommate gave his full attention to a young man rejoicing in having passed his driving test on the third try. And, very often, a grandparent was always eager to put down the newspaper and listen to the child returning home from school. The listening of the other person was water to a thirsty soul, imbibed once again while the student is writing about the memory for another listening person, me.

Often the act of being listened to had cultivated hope that they mattered to someone. The listener had no agenda other than to understand and no message to communicate other than love. No "so what?" or "what next?" dismissal of the heart's outpouring. The students write of being listened to in a way that was sustaining, often in the midst of an emotionally barren environment, and the other person's listening attention became an aquifer of hope. In the Gospels this is the kind of listening we see Jesus extend repeatedly, to a blind man on the side of the road, to a distraught mother and even to a thief being executed alongside him.

The listener becomes a sounding board on which the soul's speech is sustained and amplified, gradually becoming audible. Mingling the imagery of listening and beholding, the poet William Butler Yeats wrote, "We can make our minds so like still water that beings gather about us that they may see, it may be, their own images, and so live for a moment with a clearer, perhaps even with a fiercer life because of our quiet."[8] Such reflection cultivates the health of persons and relationships.

I often read in a student's second reflection paper how listening to another stirred discovery in the listener. It is as though God speaks through the one being listened to, sometimes with a corrective insight that stretches the listener's heart, and sometimes with a word or phrase so striking to the listener that he or she feels attended to by God even while attending to the other.

As a spiritual director I experience God communicating to me as I listen to others, whether through coincidences of life experiences or simply, yet amazingly, through evidence of holy love present in human life.

THE RELIGIOUS IMPERATIVE TO LISTEN

While listening has been considered an aretogenic (or virtue-cultivating) necessity by ancient philosophers and some contemporary social scientists, it's also a religious imperative. The disciple

Peter and his friends watched in amazement one day as Jesus was joined on a mountaintop by Moses and Elijah, long-deceased Hebrew luminaries. Peter began to babble, for he "did not know what to say" (Mark 9:6), and the other disciples, wanting to be helpful and perhaps gain some sense of control, started building tents for the holy men.

However, their plans were aborted when "a cloud appeared and covered them," and they heard a voice from the cloud saying, "This is my Son, the Beloved; listen to him!" (Mark 9:7). An imperative! They were to be still and listen. Dietrich Bonhoeffer claimed that the "love of God begins with listening to His Word" and "the beginning of love for the brethren is learning to listen to them."[9] How often is our first act to listen?

The imperative to listen is underscored in Christian Scriptures by the affirmation that Jesus is the Word of God, the Word that was in the beginning with God and indeed was God. The Hebrew word used to translate "Word" in John 1:1 is the ancient *davar,* the meanings of which include "word" and "thing," and, less commonly, "order" and "purpose." We orient ourselves toward the Word to which we are listening, which then orders our life by setting our feet on the right way. This Word can be beheld and heard and, as we see in both Testaments, is like bread that can be eaten. Isaiah 55:10 tells us that the Word comes down like rain from the heavens, which waters the earth, which produces grain that can be made into bread for the people. Jesus (John 6:51) tells us that he is the Word, to be eaten. *We take the Word into us, food for walking trees.*

Jesus, the Word, said to those gathered around him, "Listen and understand" (Matthew 15:10 NIV). "Listen and understand" at all times, including when, like Peter, we are sincerely overwhelmed and confused by God's mystery.

Listening is not only our response to the Holy; it's also our *imitatio Christi,* our imitation of Christ.[10] Jesus asks us, "What do you want me to do for you?" or "What are you discussing with each other as you walk along?" He then listens for the response. The engaged posture of listening is focused, grounded and receptive, and the listener is neither performing nor spectating. There is countercultural stillness and openness in listening.

Not surprisingly, our culture values speaking over listening. We can take courses in speaking as presentation, persuasion and promotion. Seminaries offer courses in preaching, but not often in listening. Some of the highest-paid independent contractors are motivational speakers, and former corporate and national presidents are on the circuit.

There are many motivations for speaking, most of which ignore listening, pursuing neither the democratic ideal of shared speech nor the theological ideal of conversation that shapes our souls. In this listening-deprived environment, it's not surprising that we have professionals whose primary service is listening.

LISTENING CULTIVATES RELATIONSHIP

While listening may cultivate virtue, it does so through cultivating relationships, including our ever-mysterious relationship with God. God spoke creation into being, and in the beginning was the Word (*logos*; John 1:1). Creation, human beings included, has been formed by communication. Tertullian (two centuries after Jesus) and Erasmus (in the early sixteenth century) both translated the *logos* of John 1:1 as *sermo,* yielding this translation in English: "In the beginning was the conversation."[11]

Mutual listening forms our relationship with God. Scripture tells us God speaks and listens to us and knows our hearts. In Acts 1:24 and 15:8, God is referred to as a "cardionostician," and we're told that God loves those with understanding (listening) hearts (1 Kings 3:9). Yet as the prophets and Jesus pointed out, we can so fixate on our idea of God that we fail to listen to the God who is always present and communicating.

"The images topple, but the voice is never silenced."[12] We are to listen to that voice. But what exactly is listening?

LISTENING IS . . .

Intentionally Attentive. Listening "is engaged hearing. Its social equivalent in the visual sphere is the experience of eyes meeting and the sense that this produces of being involved in a communicational contract."[13] A relational understanding takes place based on attunement and reattunement, like the attentive care required in a garden. We listen and listen again, homing in on what is really being communicated.

Listening requires intention and directionality.[14] The first act of listening is to direct our attention to the other. Jesus stopped and turned toward the woman at the well in order to listen to her. When we listen to another person, we must first stop and turn. Then possibly sit down. The other person needs to see our listening.

Listening involves attention within a moral and existential realm of significance, because some things matter more than others and therefore attract one's attention. For example, a person tells a long story of the week's activities, and suddenly the word *hope* catches the listening friend's attention. Here is something new, maybe important, possibly a thread that leads to a deeper place. The listener turns toward that mentioned hope. Listening is neither passive nor neutral, and it opens us to the possibility of the unexpected.

Relational. Listening is about relating, so whether we listen to another's voice or read lips or sign language, communication, not its mode, is crucial. Mere hearing does not entail a communicational intent. We hear in the circuses of our lives, be it the television, the freeway sounds or the obscuring noise suffusing our places of work. We hear the phone ring, but we listen to the person.

In spiritual listening, the orientation toward the other involves care. When we listen to another person in the stance of care, relating is the foremost concern. We invite the other into a listening shelter of kindness. Listening—more than any suggestion, story or advice given as response—is the greatest gift we can offer.

The *logos*, who was in the beginning, is not only the ordering word that is spoken but also the person who cares. Martin Heidegger considered it problematic that *logos* had been defined as expression only and pointed to an early Greek understanding of the word that has to do with that which is laid down, laid before, brought together, gathered and sheltered.[15] This is garden-like imagery that adds relational care to the starkness of doctrine. Even before God spoke creation into being, the Spirit hovered over the darkness with sheltering care (Genesis 1:2).

The Word to whom we listen listens to us and guides us. The Word and the Way are one. This is compatible with scriptural understandings of leadership, like gardening and shepherding. The Word who cares for us is also to be heeded. The sheep know the sound of the Shepherd's voice, the particular Shepherd who seeks out each sheep and whose way of leading is one of "constant, individualized and final kindness."[16]

God is kind but not passive. Heidegger claims that true *logos* is like lightning, part of the "storm of Being."[17] So too "the voice of the LORD is over the waters; the God of glory thunders" (Psalm 29:3). Today we try to manage thunderstorms through cloud seeding and storm dispersal. Spiritual thinking can become similarly managerial. When we close our hearts to the Word's relational mystery and power, we miss out on the sheltering kindness—and the lightning.

Responsively Attuned. The embodied, textured liveliness of relationship is essential to any real communication, and that requires attentiveness and attunement. Our son Andrew relies on sign language interpreters in speaking environments. Excellent interpreters transmit more than the words alone, and in worship services I have watched my son's interpreter Christine Hearn convey such depth of meaning while signing Scripture that the entire congregation oriented itself toward her. She was attuned to the full emotional and existential breadth of what was read, and she was also attuned to those watching her. As words flowed through her body and heart, we in the congregation who had heard the words so often that our ears were dull found them come alive again. From her expressive hands, we received God's Word into our hearts and minds.

"Belonging together always also means being able to listen to one another,"[18] and this is so even in healthy adversarial relationships, such as we find in politics, the academy, the courts and certain scriptural prayers (consider some of David's psalms and Job's protest). If we have not accurately heard the other in an adversarial situation, we begin our argument on shifting ground. Millennia ago Heraclitus wrote something similar: "Knowing not how to listen, they know not how to speak."[19] This is even the case in adversarial conversation in which compassionate identification is not an undergirding ideal.

When we listen to another person, we follow the flow of the communication, correcting, turning and attuning our listening as new terrain is explored. When we are listened to in such a way, our hearts open before God.

FROM MERCY FLOWS JUSTICE: AN ILLUSTRATION

In 2011 a powerful witness to the transforming grace of listening appeared in a newspaper article about Ghana. For a decade public health workers there had worked to promote family planning in order to curb overpopulation and prevent the spread of the HIV virus, but they had met with only limited success. Then they began to notice that women in the Kassena-Nankana district in the north part of the country were starting to have smaller families, independent of whether they lived near the programs that were encouraging family planning.

At the same time, the researchers noticed that a large number of evangelical preachers were establishing churches in this part of the Ghanaian hinterlands, and many women were attending the Sunday services. The researchers found that the female Christian converts were three times as likely to use family planning as were women who maintained their traditional African worldview.

The article went on to state that Kassena-Nankana women traditionally are excluded from everyday decision making, even in the home, and are forbidden to communicate with spirits. But the "born-again" women were forming committees, making speeches and becoming involved in civic life.

Moreover, the Christian women were speaking directly to Jesus about their problems. The journalist wrote that Jesus "was, many of them may have felt, the first man ever to listen. This may have given them a language for speaking to mortal men as well, even about such sensitive matters as contraception."[20]

Imagine that—a God who listens. A God who welcomes women, Chinese immigrant restaurant workers and first-century fishermen. God enters into conversation with them and with us. The garden becomes visible, and seeds stir to life under God's cultivating care. In the beginning was the conversation. The voice is never silenced but continues to speak. We can choose to listen—or not.

FOR REFLECTION

1. Remember a time you were listened to, and enter into the memory with your imagination. What blessings do you discover?

2. Consider the transfiguration of Jesus and ponder how you would have responded. Take God's command "Listen!" as an invitation to you when you are in prayer.

3. Think about the liberating, world-changing experience the Ghanaian Christian women had as a result of being in conversation with God. Reflect on the ways your conversations with God transform you and the world around you.

4

STOPPING

*Hear this, O Job; stop and consider
the wondrous works of God.*

JOB 37:14

M Y PARENTS LOVED HAWAII. It was the place they took
their first real vacation as a couple ten years after they
became parents, and their last time in the islands was when they
were in their eighties and my sons were young adults.

During that final visit we stayed at a wheelchair-accessible
condo on Maui's Kahana bay, where my mother spent days sitting
outside, happily drinking in the beauty of water and sky. My father
loved swimming, but his lean body had lost buoyancy and strength,
so my husband and I and our sons Peter and Andrew helped him
stay afloat while Mom watched. The young adults spent days exploring the island, and all of us gathered each evening for dinner
on the small lanai facing the beach and the western sky. Strong
personalities often generated conversational vigor.

Saturday evening we lingered at the table as darkness enveloped
us. It had been a challenge to get everyone together and all the food

transported outside, and so, like Martha of Bethany, encumbered by serving, I was irritated. Though the sun's setting marked the start of my weekly sabbath, I didn't mention it or feel its peace.

Our dinner candles glowed beneath the shadowy shapes of rain-damp palm trees swaying in the humid breeze. We fell silent. My eyes adjusting to the darkness, I could see the line dividing water from sky, a barely discernible horizontal shift in tone rising from deep black to charcoal.

BEGINNING TO STOP

As the weight of night fell, I began to notice something above the horizon that was neither star nor moon. The moon rising behind us in the east wasn't visible, yet something ever so pale glowed in the west, pricking my awareness every time I turned from it. The aurora borealis crossed my mind, incongruous as that seemed in the mid-Pacific. Whatever was there vanished when I focused my eyes in its direction. In a college astronomy class I had learned that to pay attention to faint objects in the night sky, it helps to look out of the corner of the eye where the light-sensitive rods dominate, undistracted by the color-sensitive cones at the eye's center. I played at doing that.

I drew the others' attention to the elusive light, and some couldn't see it at all. We extinguished the candles, allowing our eyes to adapt to the darkness. Finally, even straight on, we all could see what none of us knew existed: a night rainbow. It arced above the horizon like strings of luminous cobwebs or a ghostly lyre, its silvery strands pulsing, the top one most vividly as the brightness of the whole ebbed downward into the sea. Hushed by its presence, we sat there for a long time.

I've since read that night rainbows are caused by a moon close to the horizon in the opposite sky from the bow, its light shining through raindrops. Given that moonlight itself is reflected from sunlight, a moonbow is a double transmission of light to us—from sun to moon to the water drops in the sky. Darkness is required. And so are people who are in enough darkness to develop night vision.

A rainbow features in the biblical account of Noah, who, after the flood, was given one as a sign of God's promise to him and his descendants. As far as I know, no moonbow is mentioned in Scripture, but the one at Kahana became part of our family's story. As my parents approached the end of their lives, we registered a sense of promise—not the bright rainbow promise at the start of a journey but a lambent pattern of light on darkness, an affirmation straddling the horizon even at journey's end.

That the light was doubly reflected meant something too. Though we didn't see the sun or moon, light reached us, just as God's grace so often seems to come through successive mediations. It flows from someone's direct encounter, to their creation and telling of a story. Listeners, then, receive and transmit the story to other listeners for whom its grace just may reverberate. That night the grace from sun to moon to bow moved me, as does my telling about it now.

As the bow faded, tears came to my eyes. Seeing my response, my mother placed her hand on mine. The evening's friction was vanquished by the beauty we witnessed. The visitation held us all in a sheltering bow of blessing.

The night rainbow was sheer gift. We stopped, hushed and opened ourselves to the mystery of the evening. In the Hebrew Scriptures, King Hezekiah asks God to forgive the people for creating a Passover celebration that isn't quite perfectly executed, just as our sabbath dinner that evening lacked the graciousness that we might have observed. In his prayer the king tells God that the worshipers deserved blessing, for they had "set their hearts to seek

God" (2 Chronicles 30:19). That's what we can do. That night on Maui, I stopped and my heart reoriented itself toward God.

As my night vision improved, I attuned myself to deeper realities than those I'd been tripping over in the rush of meal preparation. Sabbath keeping is a time-honored way of setting our hearts to seek God, but I hadn't been doing that. Caught up in the work of the meal, I'd scarcely noticed the sunset and was only vaguely aware of the week's end. The moonbow ushered in the sabbath for me.

Sabbath had begun, and it continued. The next morning my husband and I worshiped at a small church in the neighborhood. The Filipino-Hawaiian service was mostly in Tagalog, and kind people helped us follow the words of the hymns. After preaching, the pastor asked the two of us to come forward and introduce ourselves. We told them the story of the night rainbow. Awe still held us, and the congregation caught its whiff. The grace we had received flowed through us and was amplified by their response.

COMING TO A STOP

That night on Maui, we stopped. Sabbath is one form of regular stopping, embedded in religious tradition and spiritual wisdom. Stopping is just about the most countercultural action we can take in a culture that valorizes total work. We have become increasingly unfamiliar with true stopping and deep resting. We know about the sleep mode on our computers, the snooze setting on our alarm clocks and the vegging mode of our nonwork hours, but we have little familiarity with true stopping.

What helps us stop? I regularly light one candle at the beginning of every spiritual direction hour as a reminder that the Light of the world is with us. When people stop in the chair across from me, they often discover what is going on inside them. One person told me, "I feel like a robot. I go about my days executing the tasks before me. I barely notice anything else. I fear stopping because then I will feel regret for the emptiness of my days."

Things will rise from the depths. As we stop, we will encounter what has been outside of our range of vision, beneath consciousness, perhaps intimated only intuitively.

A person engaged in ministry that gives life to many people said, "I feel flat. I have no idea what I really feel. No idea what God might be saying or doing. I'm just going through the motions—effectively and happily. But I feel cut off from what's deeper." Busyness and boredom may lurk in the shallows of our experience, separating us and possibly shielding us from deeper verities.

What's it like when you stop, sit down, take a deep breath and look around you? What do you see, smell, feel, hear, taste? Does the culture's anesthesia wear off? In the poem "Wild Geese," Mary Oliver writes that we don't have to engage in difficult ascetic practices. We just need to let the embodied, sensory self that we are "love what it loves," and in that we are restored to our "place in the family of things."[1]

We read in Genesis 2:2-3 that God stopped too. "By the seventh day God had finished the work he had been doing; so on the seventh day he rested from all his work. Then God blessed the seventh day and made it holy" (NIV). This is the first appearance of the word *holy*—*qadosh*—in Scripture. Like God, we are to stop regularly and rest from our doing, good and necessary though much of it may be.

Jesus shows us this stopping motion time and again. Going through Jericho with his disciples, Jesus heard Bartimaeus calling to him from the side of the road, and he stopped. He often stopped in the midst of all kinds of urgent interests and affairs, even in the terrifying wildness on the evening of his arrest.

Stopping enables us to register presence and possibility. It's risky to open ourselves to what our galloping lives have kept us from noticing. We may encounter darkness, and in it possibly a glimmer of light. Stopping allows us to be in touch with all that we are, all the parts of ourselves that get suppressed while our "executive" self-directing function commandeers our daily life for the sake of productivity and efficiency. We discover ourselves and are restored to our place, as it were, in the garden of the Holy One.

There is a growing cultural awareness—not necessarily associated with religious beliefs and practices—that we need to stop. Stopping may be an occasion for renewal, for the resetting of our energy-depleted brain, for mindfulness or just for the experience of stopping itself. Some people today recommend the practice of "self-binding," as Odysseus did by lashing himself to the mast to resist the Sirens' song.[2] In the absence of masts and ropes, people are finding other ways to stop. One method is an Internet app for Macs called "Freedom," which blocks Internet access for up to eight hours at a stretch—another reminder that technology offers spiritual possibilities as well as challenges.

We can enter times of stopping in other ways too, and some of these ways are involuntary. One of my directees says that it's usually illness that stops her, though she'd like to find less extreme causes for slowing down. James Kugel, an Orthodox Jew, a professor of Hebrew literature and a cancer survivor, wrote that "in the modern West . . . we shuffle through our days. . . . [Our soul] has become a strangely stunted and sealed organ, the product of the harsh environment in which it has been forced to develop."[3] In the forced stopping imposed by cancer he encountered the starkness of reality, his previously overlooked body, the people he loved and the late afternoon sun.

Kugel was thrust out of his robotic state of "shuffling" through life, possibly of measuring out his life with coffee spoons and emails. He was moved into what Josef Pieper called the kind of "silence which is the prerequisite of the apprehension of reality."[4]

THE EXTENDED STOP: FALLOWNESS

Sometimes in spiritual direction I hear about sought and unsought seasons of stopping that people describe as "fallow." Fallowness implies emptiness—intentional or not—for the sake of replenishment, and in that there is hope.

Some people experience fallowness when the way ahead is unclear: Perhaps schooling is completed but a career track hasn't materialized, or a job long held has come to an end and no new engagement is on the horizon. Maybe children have left home, and a parent has entered a liminal time of waiting for a calling. Sometimes illness or disability thrusts one into starkness, wondering what the next commitment will be. Churches, too, seem to go through seasons of fallowness. There is a stop, and in it the hope of something new ahead.

I accompanied a friend through such a time of quiet reflection. It wasn't clear what it was about, but throughout that year there was a sense of mysterious promise as some aspects of life came to an end and the seeds of other desires began to stir. My friend attended to the emptiness with hope that the less full season was a threshold into another season that was being prepared by the Holy Spirit. And so it was. Within the year, the way ahead seemed clear and the promise was being realized.

Part of the Hebrew law of sabbath was *shmita* (see Leviticus 25:2-7), a year-long sabbatical in the seventh year of labor. Seldom observed through history, it has left traces in academic institutions and some churches that allow employees regular sabbatical absences from work. During the seventh year the fields were to lie fallow, free from plowing, planting, pruning and harvesting. Measures that preserved the earth—such as watering, fertilizing, weeding, spraying, trimming and mowing—were allowed, especially for the sake of the trees on the land.

Fruit that grew was freely available to anyone who found it, as the land was given a sabbath break from the social hierarchy dividing owners and laborers. Debts, too, were forgiven during that year (Deuteronomy 15:1-11). Slaves were freed; *shmita* is often translated as "release." It was to be a time of refreshment—for people, farm animals and the land.

Listening to God during such seasons is a reason for stopping. However, an unsought season of emptiness may not be refreshing but instead depressive, exhausting or even oppositional to God's grace, and in those cases corrective action might be needed.

Choosing occasional fallowness in order to listen to God is an action that can prevent debilitating depletion. Many of the people I work with in spiritual direction have regular retreat practices. Once or twice a year they leave their home and work in order to spend time being open to receiving whatever grace might come. Some of them tell me they have to be completely alone to really come to a stop; otherwise their minds focus on the people with them. Some say they have to be in silence; any speaking interferes with their own deep listening to their souls and to God. Seasoned retreatants may know just what environment is most conducive for opening their hearts, and they seek those places. But more than mountain lakes or silence, what retreatants require is *stopping*. Then the fields of our lives that we steadfastly plow, plant and reap can lie open to the elements. What is under the surface can emerge too.

PILGRIMAGE AS FALLOWNESS

I recently walked the Camino to Santiago de Compostela in Spain with friends and family. There are a number of roads to the cathedral in Santiago, a place of Christian pilgrimage for more than a thousand years. We walked there from Porto, Portugal, a journey of more than a hundred miles and about ten days on foot.

Many people have written about the spiritual discipline of pilgrimage and the blessings associated with it. They write about simplicity, of needing only the few things you carry with you, and the gradual realization of how much unnecessary stuff we carry in ordinary life. There is also the experience of hospitality from and toward fellow pilgrims and from the people living along the Camino who for generations have extended kindness to those passing by. There is the awareness of creation and God's willingness to enter into it as a Person who spent much time walking on roads with people who were seeking grace.

I too received those blessings of the journey. Yet, as people say, we all have our own *caminos*, and mine included an experience of fallowness. As a regular sabbath keeper I recognized the freedom I felt day after day on the trail, even though I was exerting effort (more physical effort than I'm used to!) and heading toward a destination. Ironically, ten days of walking allows for a profound sense of stopping. Electronic gadgets were abandoned. No work was possible, and no multitasking. My habitual thrust-forward posture toward the next item on my to-do list was broken. I felt each step, and my mind didn't go much further than the next one.

Most of my time is spent indoors. The pilgrimage kept me in the landscape, on rainy days and hot, sunny ones. I noticed the texture of the dirt and stones on the road. I noticed my body, instead of just what was on my mind. Usually technology allows us to be effectively bionic—traversing territory while encased in steel, contacting people at a distance via devices and cooking food in minutes without employing visible fuel. On the trail we were merely human: all biology, no electronics. Occasionally my biological self cried out in blistering protest, but on the whole my body was my friend, cooperating with the task before it and carrying me ever forward.

Free of any mental project while I walked five or six hours at a stretch, thoughts and feelings that find little space in daily life at home were able to surface in the openness of my mind. The usual barrier between unconscious and conscious thinned as my walking sticks rhythmically pierced the ground.

Some thoughts were triggered by the physical experience itself. In a whole body way I remembered being a child with sun on my legs and dirt crunching under my shoes. College backpacking trips sprang to mind. My younger self was a companion on the road, and she doesn't often get much conscious airtime. I thought, too, about Jesus' body and how long before his feet were anointed or pierced; they were dirty and calloused.

Relationships moved in and out of my awareness, especially as I was accompanied by people I love. Some days we spread out along the road, making progress out of sight of one another, the way we ordinarily journey through our interlocking yet separate lives. My imagination went to others who have been my companions through the years, some of them—like my parents—no longer reachable yet still so intimately a part of me. And as I trod in ancient footsteps, my heart expanded toward the whole communion of saints.

As the days wore on, I also felt regret for some paths not taken, relationships that cooled or broke, and for paying so little attention to the earth, to my body, to the steady movements of seasons and years, and to feelings within me that deserve to be given attention. As I walked, those regrets rose up in a poignant mingling of confession and acceptance. It felt like God's cultivation of my soul.

Nature's vivid presence—including the bit of it that I am—made me marvel that I ever ignore it. With that awareness came the desire to notice it more and more, for there will come a day when my relationship to it is radically altered, and I won't stamp on a trail or breathe in the sweet air of a nearby vineyard. Long hours passed in the pilgrimage's fallow space, during which I followed Jesus' command to consider lilies and the birds of the air: emptiness for the sake of replenishment.

STOPPING FOR HOLY LISTENING: AN ILLUSTRATION

A circuslike culture interferes with practices of stopping, and even committed sabbath keepers find the practice challenging and solitary. Few communal practices of stopping remain, yet occasionally whole societies choose to pause for a season in order to heal, reorder hierarchies and seek communal forgiveness.

In 1995, as apartheid was ending and democracy beginning in South Africa, the people held hearings on those charged with human rights violations committed between 1960 and 1994. Unlike the Nuremburg Trials following World War II, these hearings were focused on truth telling, listening and reconciliation. They were not criminal trials. The Truth and Reconciliation Commission's (TRC) explicit mandate was to bear witness to and record crimes relating to human rights violations, as well as to effect reparation and rehabilitation, and in some cases to grant amnesty to the perpetrators.

The watching world stopped and listened too, bearing witness to the suffering so many people had endured. Those who listened, including the victims, were changed in the process. One victim of South African apartheid, Mzukisi Mdidimba, testified before the TRC about severe beatings he had received in solitary confinement when he was fifteen years old. After testifying, Mdidimba said, "When I have told stories of my life before, afterward I am crying, crying, crying." But this time he knew that people all over the country were listening over radios and televisions. Knowing that people, seen and unseen, stopped what they were doing and paid attention affected the victims. Being heard made a difference, such that "I still have some sort of crying, but also joy inside."[5] When Mdidimba's grief was heard, joy was released.

Some of those who testified before the TRC experienced healing that was manifested in various ways: a greater ability to return to normal work, daily activity and sleep; less fear and anger toward offenders; increased compassion for the offenders; a greater sense of security and trust in the world in general; greater self-confidence and less anxiety. The reconciliation process acknowledged the fact that tragedy can never be undone and will always remain. There will be loss and scarring. But even so, for some of those involved, the practice of stopping, speaking and listening fostered healing that flows in the world.

An intriguing feature of the TRC hearings in South Africa was that they included religious leaders as well as statespersons, so spiritual matters—even reverence—were part of the conversation.[6] A journalist wrote,

> "Today," said an old Black man, "the nation cried my tears with me." . . . This potentiality is undoubtedly aided by the person who is chair, Desmond Tutu. He has wept with the victims and marked every moment of repentance and for-giveness with awe. Where a jurist would have been logical, he has not hesitated to be theological. He has sensed when to lead audience members in a hymn to help a victim recover composure and when to call them all to prayer.[7]

The bishop's and the nation's tears reverenced the man's suffering.

Bishop Tutu allowed the people's stories to run through his heart, and he let everyone see that. He brought people to a holy stop, lending compassion to the process and marking it with awe.

He was the walking tree of Scripture, planted by streams of living water and walking the way of truth. He cooperated with the divine *Logos* that shelters and gathers as well as speaks.

Holy listening contrasted starkly with the violence that scarred South Africa in earlier years when, as in a macabre circus, a few people wielded power while others were stripped of personhood, subjected to nonrecognition and brutalized. Many South Africans and others, morally anesthetized, had merely observed the spectacle.

In the best moments of the gardenlike space crafted by the TRC, people were beheld in their wholeness. Time slowed. The whole truth was welcomed. Conversations about humanity at its worst were met with listening and prayer.

Mercy and truth have met together;
Righteousness and peace have kissed. (Psalm 85:10-11 NKJV)

STOPPING TO RECEIVE

Philosopher Hans-Georg Gadamer wrote that genuine relationships are built on openness, and "anyone who listens is fundamentally open."[8] Think about opening your mouth and drinking. Doesn't it help to pause first? Opening our hearts requires an existential stopping too. When we make that movement, we can take in what is offered, which, in the case of South Africa's Truth and Reconciliation Commission, were stories very hard to tell and to hear.

Listening sets up the possibility of acknowledgment, a process that entails critical self-consciousness, openness, responsiveness and a capacity for guilt, shame, grief, regret and, as Bishop Tutu displayed, reverence. Fallow seasons of stopping allow for the healing process of acknowledgment, as I experienced in the confession that arose in me on pilgrimage.

Acknowledgment is moral work. Spiritually, it allows a "long, loving look at the real," an act of reverence and contemplation.[9] It is a way of working through the past, an alternative to our circuslike culture's polarized options of forgetting and, alternatively, ceaselessly striving toward mastery. The cultivation of the society's health depends on the courage and discipline of particular individuals, like Bishop Tutu, who practice the discipline of stopping in order to listen with humble, open hearts.

Writing about South Africa's TRC and drawing on the work of philosophers writing in the years following the European Holocaust, journalist Susie Linfield argued that acknowledgment "is nurtured simultaneously in political and psychic realms," "demands moral and systemic change," "can be accomplished only by individuals, yet only within a collective," and "demands a rigorous scrutiny of the soul."[10] John Borneman, an anthropologist who studies societies ravaged by genocide, has written that practices of listening are the most essential elements in reconstructing the social order and enabling reconciliation that is real and lasting.[11] Any morally or spiritually significant conversation must be preceded and followed by listening.

Stopping and listening are spiritual disciplines that lay a foundation for healing, even for those who have suffered great affliction. Here, as in all spiritual disciplines, God's grace flows to persons and through them to the world.

Jesus stopped the action on the Emmaus road, enabling his companions to experience what was beneath their conscious awareness as it came in contact with the grace of Jesus' presence. On Maui with my parents, stopping for the sabbath enabled me to open in such a way that the beauty of creation touched the depths of my soul, depths which had previously been obscured by surface irritations and busyness. Bishop Tutu and others brought a whole country to its knees, a resolute stop for the sake of contrition and reconciliation. Stopping is soul work.

FOR REFLECTION

1. Stopping is a spiritual discipline. Do you stop regularly? When you think about stopping, what practice comes to mind? Consider the fruit that stopping bears in your life.

2. When, if ever, did you experience fallowness, an emptiness that allows for refreshment?

3. Communal practices of stopping are rare. Does your community stop for the sake of healing, forgiveness or a reordering of hierarchies?

5

SABBATH KEEPING

We thank Thee for our little light,
that is dappled with shadow.

T. S. ELIOT, CHORUSES FROM *THE ROCK*

A PHYSICIST FRIEND OF MINE recently went on his first cruise. Having lived all his life in cities, he wanted to see what the stars looked like far from the lights of land. At night somewhere in the Caribbean, he prowled the decks of the ever-partying ship, straining to see the night sky. Ultimately he gave up. Nowhere on the decks was he able to see beyond the glare of the brightly lit ship. Stars, it turned out, were better seen from his home on a quiet street in Oakland.

My friend may have been on a Carnival cruise, but, even if not, it was a spectacle. His story is a kind of parable: We marshal our resources in an effort to see more clearly, and sometimes what's needed is stillness, coming to a stop. Sometimes that possibility is close at hand, in our own home and on our weekly calendar.

STOP! IN THE NAME OF LOVE

Since 1965 millions of people around the world have listened to Diana Ross and the Supremes sing "Stop! In the Name of Love," their right hands raised in a universal gesture commanding the observer to halt. The Hebrew word *shabbat* means stop, cease, rest and, as a command issued by God, is a stop in the name of Love.[1]

Now it's quite possible that Ross and her colleagues were not singing about sabbath keeping, but the song's title expresses the invitation I believe God is extending to all of us.[2] It's a call to a radical practice—radical (like radish) in the sense that it roots and grounds us in God's grace, and also radical (as in the Sixties) in that it challenges the prevailing culture. Stop in the name of love. Stand down from work and usefulness. Attend to the Lord. Desist from distraction. Sabbath keeping helps us stop.

Sabbath keeping is a radically anticircus spiritual discipline, for the illusion of circus is that it, like the contemporary marketplace, never stops. In 2009 the *Harvard Business Review* called jobs that require seventy-hour workweeks the new standard for professionals, and *Fortune* magazine announced that the sixty-hour workweek was part time.[3] Even people who work fewer hours are engulfed by work consciousness.

In 1948 Josef Pieper presciently warned against succumbing to the ethos of "total work," advocating leisure as a refreshing abstinence from work.[4] But many of us find there are few clear boundaries between the kinds of work we do and other areas of our lives. Moreover, too little of our leisure time is truly refreshing.

As a spiritual director I hear people speak about the rare and precious joy of going on vacation to locations so remote that they're actually off the grid. I've read that the Post Ranch in Big Sur—a notably quiet part of the California coastline—offers cliff-top rooms without televisions for $2,285 a night.[5] Silence is golden in our culture; stopping, a rare pleasure.

Trailblazers in the contemporary Protestant spiritual formation movement, such as Richard Foster and Dallas Willard, did not include sabbath keeping in their lists of spiritual disciplines thirty years ago. Since that time, however, Christians have been giving the practice more attention, possibly in response to a culture that's growing increasingly circuslike. In 2011 I spoke about spiritual disciplines to the faculty of the Evangelical Theological Seminary in Cairo, Egypt. The country was in the throes of revolution, and what the professors most wanted to discuss with me was the faith-anchoring practice of sabbath keeping.

Pope Francis, speaking for a tradition that has been less committed to the sabbath than some other traditions have been, has taken a stand in favor of sabbath keeping: "More and more people work on Sundays as a consequence of the competitiveness imposed by a consumer society." In such cases, he concluded, "work ends up dehumanizing people."[6]

Jesus claimed that the sabbath is made for people, and that, as a matter of fact, he is Lord of the sabbath (Mark 2:27). Sabbath reminds us that the world is God's, not ours.

THE GIFT OF SABBATH

The gift of sabbath, like all gifts, requires disciplines of receiving that help us open our hands and hearts. I sometimes invite groups of people to close their eyes while extending an open hand. I then circulate among them placing some small object—usually a seed or chocolate—on each person's palm. It's an exercise in receptivity, opening up in the presence of another who cares for you, just as we do before God in prayer.

Many of my students and retreatants are caregivers—teachers, ministers, nurses, parents, physicians, therapists. Often they're so used to being in the caregiver posture that they're a bit rusty at the practice of opening their own hands or hearts before another. Most people express gratitude or relief when they open their eyes and see the gift. A few of them talk about the fears and discomfort the exercise evoked: "Will she put something unpleasant in my hand?" No. "Will she pass me by?" Never. "When will this awkward exercise end?!" No telling.

Gifts are relational, and like all Christian spiritual disciplines, sabbath keeping is too. A complex feeling-bond develops between us and the one who gives to us. As with some of the students who extended their hands to me, receiving can leave us feeling uncomfortably exposed and vulnerable. Sabbath keeping is important not only because it is commanded or because it is a habit of highly effective (or piously religious) people. It cultivates our bond with the loving One who says, "Be still, and know that I am God" (Psalm 46:10).

Our culture's preferred mode is anything but still. Constant work generates the impression of control and efficiency, holding at bay the mysterious while suppressing awareness of our own uncomfortable finitude. How much defensiveness against discomfort underlies both the neglect of sabbath keeping *and* the strict sabbath keeping that dodges relationship by focusing on rules and prohibitions?

Acknowledging sabbath as gift helps us focus on what's important. Susanna Wesley did so in the early 1700s when she was subjected to questions about whether "the severity of the Jewish Sabbath is remitted under the Christian economy."[7] Wesley, who is known as the "Mother of Methodism" and sometimes had as many as two hundred people worshiping in her home, received the sabbath as a gift from God. Wisely, she chose not to enter the theological debates surrounding sabbath, instead opting "to bless and praise our God for giving us leave to enjoy a Sabbath, for permitting us to refresh our souls by a view of that rest and glory which he hath prepared for those that love him."[8] And how she needed that refreshment! A woman who bore nineteen children, Wesley famously tossed her apron over her head to achieve the silence and solitude she sought, forever endearing her to parents who wonder how on earth they can keep the sabbath.

KEEPING THE SABBATH HOLY: FOUR MOVEMENTS

Scripture invites us to receive the gift of sabbath and offers practical wisdom for doing so. One of the most succinct and helpful sets of sabbath guidelines can be found in Isaiah 58.

Through the prophet Isaiah the Hebrew people were asked to seek justice for the poor and were promised that when they acted as God wishes, they (read "we") would be "like a watered garden," restored and nourished (Isaiah 58:11). Following those instructions and that promise, Isaiah turned to sabbath keeping, describing the movements of the heart involved in honoring the day of the Lord:

> If you refrain from trampling the sabbath,
>> from pursuing your own interests on my holy day;
> if you call the sabbath a delight
>> and the holy day of the LORD honorable;
> if you honor it, not going your own ways,
>> serving your own interests, or pursuing your own affairs;
> then you shall take delight in the LORD,
>> and I will make you ride upon the heights of the earth;
> I will feed you with the heritage of your ancestor Jacob,
>> for the mouth of the LORD has spoken. (Isaiah 58:13-14)

This good news is extended to us. Grace will flow, saturating our souls, and then flow through us to the world, such that the "light shall break forth like the dawn" (Isaiah 58:8).

STOP

The NRSV translation of this Isaiah passage about sabbath begins with the word *refrain*, which comes from the Latin word (*refrenare*) for stopping a horse with a bridle. This is apt, for sabbath can feel like a bridle arresting us in the midst of our full-gallop life. What helps us stop? Every Friday at dinnertime as the sun goes down, many Jewish women light candles for their families and pray, "Blessed are you, Lord our God, King of the universe, who has set us apart by his commandments and commanded us to kindle the Sabbath lights."[9] While the sun descends below the horizon, I've had the privilege of watching friends light the two Shabbat candles, which signify the two biblical mentions of Shabbat law (Deuteronomy 5:12-15 and Exodus 20:8-11).

Sabbath links creation and eternity, and that reality may be dimly apprehended as we stop and turn toward God. Abraham Joshua Heschel, the renowned rabbi and theologian, ended his gem of a book *The Sabbath* with the sentence "Eternity utters a day."[10] In the moment of stopping, we savor the beginning of time and have a foretaste of the eternal. We are humbled, grounded and watered. Wonder and awe become possible. So do confession and reformation.

Sabbath time is radically countercultural in our secular age of quantifiable time. The word *secular* means that which is embedded in ordinary time, from *saeculum*, a century or age, a unit of time that is measurable.[11] Sabbath counters the efficiency and profit-seeking commodification that renders time as money with all the associated costs and benefits, use and waste, investment and loss. Secular time, *chronos* or chronological time, is described by the philosopher Charles Taylor as ordinary, empty, homogenous, transitive, dispersed, horizontal, sequenced and measured. With what do you measure out your life? Posts, blogs, tweets, laps, spinning intervals, margins, activity units . . . ?

Sabbath time is unmeasured. In both the busy efficiency and the vacant relaxation modes of our lives, we've lost our understanding of *kairos*—immeasurable, qualitative—time, the opposite of secular time. Yet we long for its sanctity. Sabbath exists in this higher time, which is gathered and held—rather than measured and utilized— by God. We are invited to enter it. Taylor refers to this immeasurable time with a variety of adjectives—*eternal, knotted, gathered, higher, vertical, hallowed, liminoid, full*—each offering a different view of what's ineffable.

To enter sabbath time is to join God in hallowed time. Sabbath is intimately relational. The faithful are enjoined to "remember the Sabbath-day to sanctify it" (Exodus 20:8 YLT), and the Hebrew phrase for sanctify, *le-kadesh,* is the same expression found in the Talmud for consecrating or betrothing a woman to a man. We repledge our troth to God as sabbath arrives.

This is to say that sabbath is covenantal. In Ezekiel (20:12-13 and chapter 21) God speaks of having given people the sabbath as a sign of holy covenant, but the people desecrated the sabbath, and in doing so lost their understanding of God. The relationship was defiled, inheritance and salvation were lost. Later, God as Jesus entered historical time, thus sacralizing ordinary time.

We may enter sacred time by participating in God's life,[12] and a time-honored way of doing so is by keeping the sabbath day holy. While sabbath is gift, it also is a ritual that reminds us of creation and eternity. As the earth turns toward the dusk of sabbath, we stop and remember God.

Turn From

When we stop, we notice that from which we're turning. On the street where I live there's a stop sign situated at the bottom of a downhill slope. Cars come upon it suddenly, around a bend. In our soccer-mom days, my friends and I used to laugh about how we would slam on the brakes as we came upon the stop sign, all our kids' sports gear catapulting forward from nether regions of the car. When we stop for sabbath or in fallowness, we discover our baggage.

Stopping, we might, like the people on the Emmaus road, notice an upwelling of confusion, hope, fear, questions, sadness and also our longing for God. We may notice within us what amounts to weeds in need of pruning and tendrils in need of tending by the Gardener of our soul.

We keep the sabbath and "call it a delight" as we cease our trampling and shuffling about. We keep the commandment and receive the gift, possibly from sundown to sundown. There have been disputes in the church as to the sabbath's content, scheduling, theological import and eschatological referent. Nevertheless, Scripture, biblical example and the tradition of faith invite us to observe an entire day of stopping each week. God stopped for a day.

Framing the sabbath between two settings of the sun distinguishes sabbath keeping from many spiritual disciplines, allowing nature to hold the structure rather than requiring us to do so for ourselves. With most of our disciplines, we set the time frame and strive to hold to it. When life interferes, we can negotiate with disciplines. For example, "though I usually pray and write in my journal in the morning, today I have early meetings, so I'll pray tonight." We may or may not honor that deferred commitment.

But a sabbath signaled by the setting of the sun simply *arrives*. God's holy day beckons to us. If we accept it, we're moved into the rhythm of nature—the sun's journey through the sky, the changing fragrances as the earth heats and cools, and the too often obscured experience of our bodily sensations in response to that sensuous world. This is garden time. We can decline the invitation to enter the sabbath, but it has begun.

Abraham Heschel declared that for the Jews, "the Sabbaths are our great cathedrals . . . neither the Romans nor the Germans were able to burn."[13] The sabbath is a temple in time. The Ten Commandments do not command building a temple or altar, nor do they command attending a worship service or participating in some of the spiritual disciplines we consider normative for people of faith. What the commandments do specify is the sanctification of the seventh day.

Heschel wrote that Jews could enter the sabbath's holy space and remember God's faithfulness wherever they were: in the desert, in exile, in labor camps, and even in times that were distractingly plentiful and productive. People have always needed this kind of architectural time for shelter from the winds of culture and the nattering of our own concerns. We need it especially now in our circuslike culture.

Consider how you sometimes slip out of the pressures of time and find shelter in spacious, holy time. I know people who have programmed their computers to sound a chime on the hour. They are using a secular tool to call themselves to holy attention. The chime invites them into a sabbath moment in which the competing demands of life are left behind and they can breathe deeply.

FORGO OUR OWN WAYS

The biblical wisdom of sabbath keeping invites us to turn from social divisions and labor on the seventh day. Laborers and employers gather as equal participants in worship and turn from the all-enveloping category of usefulness.

Receiving the gift of sabbath opposes powerful influences in our culture. Most directly, it counters our drive to find and assign legitimation entirely through work. The nonrevealing, self-legitimating and reflexive response to the question "How are you?" is no longer "Fine." In the past few years it has become "Busy." Imagine how this affects those who are sidelined from the workforce: the disabled, unemployed, retired and ill. Particularly insidious is the religious form of this view by which we are "subverted by 'angel of light' tactics . . . and consider our Sabbath breaking to be virtuous."[14] This may be a particular temptation as churches absorb the culture's valorization of constant work and the language of strategizing, leadership and entrepreneurship.

The ancient Roman reaction to the Jews' adherence to the law of abstaining from labor on the sabbath was contempt.[15] What earthly sense did it make? Some Jews legitimated the practice by referring to relaxation as a means to an end.[16] This was Aristotle's view too; he wrote that "we need relaxation because we cannot work continuously. Relaxation, then, is not an end; for it is taken for the sake of activity."[17] The biblical sabbath, however, is simply commanded; it is not justified by its usefulness. The sense it makes is heavenly.

In our culture we sometimes bemoan the need to sleep because it robs us of productive time and we see it as wasteful. We run the danger of murdering sleep, that sleep which Shakespeare praised as necessary, for it "knits up the ravell'd sleeve of care" and is the chief "nourisher in life's feast."[18] Too often we go "[our] own ways" (Isaiah 58:13), unraveled and undernourished, failing to receive the care and feast of sabbath time within the overarching possibility of garden living.

Sabbath exists outside of instrumental legitimation and economic calculation. We are to call the sabbath a delight, not a resource; a gift, not a commodity; a spiritual discipline, not a duty. Jesus five times exposes sabbath distortion as a cruel instrument of oppression and restores the sabbath to being "a gift for living in free obedience before and with God,"[19] a gift we're to receive with regularity.

We are to seek justice, free the oppressed, care for the poor, share the good news. And keep the sabbath holy.

TURN TOWARD

God hallows the sabbath; we call it "holy" and observe it as such. As we turn toward God we encounter holiness, not merely a sensory experience of peace or the pause that refreshes.

Many words in our English versions of Scripture begin with the prefix *re-*, the Latin base of which means "again." As human beings, we need to take actions repeatedly: breathe again, sleep and eat again. So, too, we need to turn again toward God who calls us to *re*pent of our wanderings—mental and otherwise—that have turned us from God. *Re*member God, *re*turn to Jesus, *re*ceive the Holy Spirit. *Re*treat from pursuing our own interests while *re*fraining from trampling the sabbath. We do these things so that, yet again, we can call the sabbath a delight and the holy day of the Lord honorable.

We step back into the cathedral of time where we hope to encounter God. As we stop, what's deepest in us becomes evident. Some things peel away: social roles, work and constant immersion in efficiency thinking. The things that remain are likely to be what are deep and true—including hopes and fears—and we bring them to God in prayer. Accepting the gift of sabbath involves dropping our guard and relinquishing the legitimating roles of worker, performer, producer and consumer. Who are we apart from those roles? God only knows.

A minister who sees me for spiritual direction says, "My mind is racing. In the space of prayer, the sanctuary of sabbath, the racing gradually ebbs and I'm left with what I experience as the core of me. I'm repentant before God and thirsty to receive whatever God would give me. I am humbled. Grateful. At rest."

Turning toward God entails a pivot movement, a reorientation. See Mary Magdalene at the tomb turning toward the gardener who calls her by name, and Peter diving off the boat and swimming to shore, eager to receive what Jesus has to offer. We see this movement as we worship. People close their eyes and turn their faces up toward God. Some persons extend their arms and open their hands. Some kneel—full stop—like Moses at the burning bush. Sabbath is holy ground. We take off our shoes, perhaps light a candle or two. What we receive may change us radically, cost us dearly, bless us immeasurably. We turn toward it, trusting the One who invites us to stay awhile.

SABBATH KEEPING IN CAPTIVITY: AN ILLUSTRATION

More than thirty years ago at the First Presbyterian Church of Berkeley, we prayed for a Presbyterian minister named Ben Weir, and fifteen years later I learned more about him when he spoke at New College Berkeley and when he wrote a memoir. We had begun praying in 1983 because Ben and his wife Carol were about to return to work in Lebanon, a country torn by nine years of civil war. In May 1984 we learned that Ben had been kidnapped by a group of Shi'ite Muslim extremists. He was held captive for sixteen months, and throughout that time we prayed for him.

During his captivity, Weir sought ways to maintain his health and spirit. One of his practices was remembering the holy day of the Lord. He prepared to stop: "Sunday would be for me a special day of worship. I decided to observe Communion, so when supper came on Saturday I set aside a piece of bread from my sandwich."[20]

When he woke the next morning, on his mind was a visit he and his wife had made to Pakistan. He remembered a Sunday with the people there, and he imagined them and others worshiping in different time zones around the world: "My mind moved westward with the sun: Assyrian, Armenian, Persian-speaking Christians in various cities of Iran, and Arabic-speaking Christians in Iraq coming to worship also. I envisioned people of various cultural backgrounds gathering at an ecumenical center in Kuwait. I was part of this far-flung family, the very body of Christ."[21] In solitary confinement, he wasn't alone. Pastor Weir's sabbath practice embedded him in the communion of saints, the body of Christ.

Weir wrote, "I unwrapped my piece of bread and began the Presbyterian order of worship: 'We are now about to celebrate the sacrament of the Lord's Supper.' . . . I ate the bread behind closed doors with the fearful disciples and the risen Lord on that first Easter. When it came to sharing the cup I had no visible wine, but that didn't seem to matter. I knew that others were taking the cup for me elsewhere at this universal table."[22]

Weir's "universal table" is akin to Heschel's description of sabbath as the "cathedral in time" where boundaries of time and place are replaced with alignments of presence and grace. Weir was in *kairos* time. As the sabbath came to a close, he remembered hymns he had listened to on Sunday evening radio broadcasts and "proceeded to have my own quiet evensong."[23] He had stopped in the name of love. In turning from the considerable concerns of his daily life, he encountered God, his beloved self and the people of God.

FOR REFLECTION

1. Some say that sabbath keeping is the most countercultural discipline we can engage in today. Because of that, we can experience great resistance—internal and external—to it. Notice and name resistances to sabbath keeping with which you are familiar.

2. There are categories of experience that we turn from when we enter sabbath (e.g., work, social roles and efficiency). What is especially difficult for you to turn from?

3. When you are able to stop, turning from other interests and engagements, what is it like to turn toward God?

6

Cultivating Attention

Listen, and hear my voice;
Pay attention, and hear my speech.

Isaiah 28:23

ATTENTION IS ESSENTIAL TO CULTIVATION. We become and discover ourselves in relation to the One who bends and comes toward us, who hovered over creation like a hen brooding on her nest (Genesis 1:2), who descended from heaven to live among us that we might turn toward God, and who is the Vinegrower caring for the branches that we are. Beneficiaries of divine attention and made in God's image, we, too, are beings who attend.

Attention in a Time of Circus Living

Circus living fragments our attention, while also fracturing interpersonal attachments. The culture in which we live shapes our health and our illness, so health patterns in a society shed light on the culture. As a graduate student I worked on part of the third edition of the *Diagnostic and Statistical Manual of the American*

Psychiatric Association (*DSM III*, published in 1980) as a member of a team of psychologists, psychiatrists and sociologists funded by the National Institute of Mental Health and focusing on the interactions between personality and social structure. A few of us were people of faith and were keenly interested in how those interactions relate to spirituality.

Hysteria and repression were no longer the dominant issues in the mental health field that they had been when contemporary psychotherapy began. Narcissistic personality disorder first appeared in the diagnostic manual of 1980, reflecting trends and conversations in the broader culture and piquing interest among those of us interested in spirituality. Also in 1980, disorders of attention and attachment made their debut in the manual and since then have moved to the forefront of social and spiritual concern.

A spirituality of cultivation fosters healthy forms of attention and attachment in a culture that is experiencing disruption of those primary human capacities. This chapter considers attention and its relation to the cultivated life and is followed by a companion chapter that offers *lectio divina* as a spiritual attentional practice. In chapter 9 attachment will be examined, followed by a chapter focusing on the attachment-cultivating practice of spiritual direction.

In spiritual direction I accompany people as they cultivate attention and attachment in spiritual ways. They wonder how they can focus on prayer in an environment that's so loud and distracting. And how can they find time to talk with friends when the demands of work leave so little time free? Coupled with the desire to grow in their relationship with God and people, there's a lament: "Our churches aren't helping us grow stronger in faith and love." Occasionally I hear an addendum to that lament: "We see lively spiritual practices from Eastern religions that give people a sense of peace and well-being. Why isn't there something like that within Christianity that can help me grow and live a more satisfying life?"

PARTICIPATING IN OUR CULTIVATION

Recently I was on a subway headed to an airport. Everyone around me was engaged with a personal electronic device, and mine was near at hand. On a billboard in the car was a *Bloomberg Business Week* ad that read, "Looking for ways to compete in the attention economy?" In our subway car, attention was held quite effectively by competitors in that economy.

Public media create a shared symbolic and narrative environment and socialize us into roles, behaviors and expectations. They receive far more of our attention than religion, school, civic life or most of our relationships. In many homes television functions as an additional member of the family or a virtual congregation, yet as an attention-getter it has met its match in the "attention economy." Encapsulated in the media circus, we become less and less aware of our own feelings, thoughts, bodies and surroundings, including the people around us.

ATTENTIONAL PRACTICES

Though concern with attention is ancient, the scientific study of it began in the nineteenth century and has now grown to the point where more than fifteen hundred articles in the field are published annually.[1] Interest in attention burgeons as, in the words of a 2014 *Time* magazine cover story, there "are no signs that the forces splitting our attention into ever smaller slices will abate."[2]

Since the middle of the last century when televisions and computers became ordinary household items, these technologies have contributed to an attentional crisis, with social media and personal communication devices operating as "weapons of mass distraction."

In the midst of the crisis, people are seeking the countervailing force of attentional practices, religious and secular, including prayer disciplines and mindfulness practice.

Various attentional practices, like meditation and mindfulness, have been employed by public institutions—hospitals, corporations, schools and the military—as ways of countering stress and discontent. Christians tell me that, knowing of few Christian practices that foster greater attention, they have taken up secular attentional practices and find them helpful.

Attentional practices expand people's abilities to notice and manage their own thoughts, feelings and behavior, a capacity often called "self-regulation," the fruit of which may include equanimity, open-mindedness and a better capacity for discernment.[3] These practices—including Christian ones, like silent prayer—fuse the opposing movements of control and release. The first act is to focus on what's on one's mind or heart. Paying attention to thoughts and feelings enables a person to release what's unwanted. In the case of silent prayer, it may take a while before the mind's chatter subsides and listening for God begins.

Attention to one's inner experience brings it to consciousness and, then, instead of being captured by the thoughts, it's possible to examine them, gain reflective distance and even make some changes. Theorists write of attentional practice as a decentering process whereby the self (or ego) and its concerns are relativized, allowing emotional composure to be achieved, at least temporarily. Many spiritual disciplines—like contemplative listening and sabbath keeping—cultivate this kind of attention, and they do so in the ultimate context of the soul's relationship with God.

We see a decentering of the ego in Christian understandings of prayer. One scholar wrote that prayer is "a wordless intimacy with radical alterity [otherness]. Prayer deconstructs *theology*; it dispossesses Self."[4] Intimacy with God helps us turn from ideas about God and also those aspects of our own self that interfere with being with God. In prayer as in sabbath keeping, we turn *from* so that we might turn *toward.*

Attentional practices of all kinds, spiritual and secular, enable us to cultivate a reflective, discerning distance from the mind's preoccupations. Peace becomes a possibility and eventually so does nonanxious action.

As a garden represents an intersection of nature and culture, so do these practices. When we turn from the noise of our lives and attend to interior experience, we recognize our own nature, notice what catches our attention and see that certain matters have a way of becoming fixed in our attention. Some of these are pleasant—hopes, plans, dreams, memories, reveries—while others are unpleasant: anxieties, worries, regrets, resentments, obsessions, grief. Some of the matters are imposed from outside of us, and some rise up from within.

The increasingly abundant and predominantly secular mindfulness literature addresses a number of these issues of attention. Looking at the main themes informs our understanding of the less-studied faith-based attentional practices, of which praying with Scripture is one example.

MINDFULNESS

In 1979 at the University of Massachusetts Medical Center, the biologist Jon Kabat-Zinn introduced an attentional protocol for the care of patients suffering from chronic pain. The practice he developed, Mindfulness Based Stress Reduction (MBSR), is now taught in more than seven hundred hospitals. In this field, techniques derived primarily from Buddhism have been secularized to help people cultivate attention.

Mindfulness is "the awareness that emerges through paying attention on purpose, in the present moment, and nonjudgmentally to the unfolding of experience moment by moment."[5] It "involves an intimate knowing of what is arising as it is arising, without trying to change or control it."[6] In addition to attentiveness, mindfulness involves a stance of accepting: nonjudgmental observation.

Kabat-Zinn says that today mindfulness is a "galloping field" that has benefited people afflicted with a variety of physical and psychological ills, as well as healthy people who are looking for less stress and more sanity in their lives.[7] Training in mindful attention to consciousness has been shown to help people change their responses to pain and stress, thus reducing their suffering,[8] and a survey of American psychotherapists showed that nearly half incorporate mindfulness practices in their clinical work.[9]

Research shows that mindfulness is dispositional (natural for certain personalities) and that it also can be acquired and strengthened through discipline. It's achievable and beneficial. In addition to their effects on consciousness and the reduction of stress, mindfulness techniques are said to yield peace, a sense of well-being, better moral decision making and possibly greater work effectiveness.

Mindfulness is defined in the academic literature in a variety of ways. One definition put forward by psychological researchers is that mindfulness is "a receptive attention to and awareness of present events and experience."[10] Contemplative space is like this, whether it's entered into by way of listening, sabbath keeping or holy reading. A spiritual directee tells me that when she remembers God in the middle of a pressured workday, she notices what is happening at the moment and becomes more aware of her body and feelings. Tensions dissipate. Gratitude wells up as she feels released from the backward tug of regret and the forward thrust of worry.

Some people today speak of "being present," as in "I was really present to my feelings as I went through that experience, which helped me make the right decision." The aim is to attend with acceptance to what is, rather than being either inattentive to it or focused solely on what has been, might be or ought to be. To cultivate a focus on what's actually present, many attentional practices begin by attuning to the body. "What are you feeling in various parts of your body as you sit? Notice your breathing . . . your heartbeat."

Some prayer practices draw attention to the sitting body, the breath and the heartbeat as people gather and sit in stillness. Such attunement can expand our awareness beyond just ourselves. Contemplative practices, like praying with Scripture, may bring to awareness the substrata of our communal, internalized experience. As we stop and are silent before the text, we may notice how our feelings exist in the context of our relationships and the culture. On the Emmaus road, Jesus helped the two people notice their thoughts and feelings before he presented them with Scripture. Then the text of Scripture met the "texts" of their open souls.

SECULAR OR SACRED?

Mindfulness is a component of many religious practices. Now that mindfulness techniques have been adopted by major secular institutions in North America and are spreading into the secular institutions of Europe, a question on the table is whether religion is a component of mindfulness.

At a time when this question was on my mind, I encountered the secular mindfulness movement in a very odd context on Good Friday of 2013. In a hotel room in the Buddhist Himalayan kingdom of Bhutan, I turned on the television, and what sprang to the screen was a BBC broadcast about mindfulness techniques being taught in British schools. The host of the show asked the panel of experts, including a Buddhist monk of European ancestry, if the movement was bringing religion into the schools. The monk responded that mindfulness, like Buddhism from which it derives, is a way of life, not a religion.

Just a few hours earlier at the cliff-hanging Tiger's Nest Monastery, I had asked an English-speaking Bhutanese Buddhist monk if Buddhism is a religion. He said, with a laugh, "Of course it's a religion!"

And, of course, a religion is a way of life. It binds together doctrines, traditions and communities, as well as practices, for the sake of knowing Life in our living—and that's what, I believe, the Bhutanese monk meant.

Stripping mindfulness practices of religious content and context allows institutions and people who are not religiously affiliated to adopt them. One journalist expressed that understanding of the practice in this way:

> In a practical sense, "sitting" is really all there is to the meditation aspect of mindfulness meditation. For anywhere from fifteen minutes to an hour (or more) each day, whether alone or with a group, you sit in a quiet place with your eyes closed, focusing on your breath as it moves in and out. Your mind will inevitably wander, which is where the mindfulness aspect comes in. Instead of growing frustrated with your lack of focus or getting caught up in the web of your thoughts, you train yourself to observe the thought or emotion with acceptance and curiosity, and to calmly bring your focus back to the breath. . . . If you strip it of its religio-historical context, mindfulness meditation is essentially cognitive fitness with a humanist face.[11]

Some scholars and practitioners who integrate Buddhism with the healing arts are concerned that crucial elements are lost in mindfulness practices when they're bereft of the traditional spiritual dimensions of wisdom (teachings, texts, as well as practices) and guidance (personal and communal).[12] What the journalist called the "religio-historical context" is the authority many people have relied on to inform their understandings of what it is to be human and good, and how we can grow in maturity.

More and more Christians—lay and clergy—report that they're attending mindfulness classes and in those classes are having lively spiritual experiences, which are, some say, more life-enhancing than their experiences in Christian contexts. One minister told me the classes are her "real church."

Our hearts desire contemplative experience, especially in our frenzied, circus-like culture, and many people are seeking practices that will cultivate it. On the whole, and in tragic contradiction to the good news of Christ, the Christian faith is not seen as the place where such contemplative experience can be found. Have we kept this light so securely under a bushel that people must seek it elsewhere? My hope is that this book removes the bushel from some of the Christian practices that have been neglected.

ATTENTION AND ITS DISCONTENTS

Contemporary secularized mindfulness practices have come on the scene at the same time that attention disorders have become among the most frequently diagnosed pathologies. Within the diagnosis of attention deficit and hyperactivity disorder, there are two forms: the predominantly inattentive-disaffected form and the predominantly hyperactive-obsessive one. The first form is marked by lethargy and fatigue, while the second is characterized by impatience and constant motion.

Some people with attention disorders move between the poles inherent in the afflictions, but both poles—the lethargic (more like "vegging") and the kinetic (like "pounding")—are inattentive. Disorders reflect cultures, and ADHD is a recognized disorder in the more economically competitive countries today.[13] While the majority of the population does not suffer from a psychiatric problem, we all struggle to be attentive in a "three-ring circus." Our culture rewards hyperactivity, competitiveness and the ability to move rapidly from one task to the next; the respite it offers is disengagement. Mindfulness practice, by contrast, offers relief from the circus by cultivating attention rather than numbing it.

First and foremost a pediatric diagnosis, and now the second most frequent long-term diagnosis in children (just after asthma), ADHD is more and more being diagnosed in adults.[14] As of 2013, 15 percent of high-school-age children in the United States had been diagnosed with the disorder. The number of children on medication for ADHD soared from 600,000 in 1990 to 3.5 million in 2013,[15] and the largest change in prescription drugs in the United States in 2011 was in ADHD drugs for women between the ages of twenty and forty-four.[16] Other countries, including China, Brazil, Canada and the United Kingdom, prefer employing psychosocial interventions with children (parent training and counseling) before resorting to medication.[17] Despite a relatively high level of comfort with medication, countries in the global North are increasingly turning to mindfulness practice as a remedy for attention disorders.

Many researchers look at the rise of diagnosis and pharmaceutical treatment as part of a drug industry campaign, but studies are also being conducted to determine the degree to which the rise in ADHD is due to social changes, such as growing levels of sleep deprivation related to our culture of constant work and connectivity.[18] Other researchers are concerned that the growing problem of childhood ADHD is related to rising income inequality in the United States and economic forces that prevent many children from receiving the parental attention they need.[19] While researchers are looking for the physiological-behavioral and socioeconomic correlates and perhaps causes of the epidemic of attention disorders, we also register its spiritual significance.

Faith-Based Attention

In its European origins, the word *attention* means to bend toward. In this there is inclination and orientation. We know another person is attending to us when the other stops, leans and turns toward us, and we see this in artistic representations of the Holy Trinity in which the three Holy Persons lean in toward one another. Theologically understood, reality is attentional in its deepest structure.

We see inclination and orientation in nature too. Trees and plants are helio- and hydrotropic: they reach toward sunlight and water. While waiting to rebloom in my kitchen, orchids need to be rotated in order to compensate for their strong leaning toward the light from the western window. Oblivious to the fact that I've placed them in a precarious position, the orchids need me to pay attention and rotate them before they topple off the shelf. Plants on the faces of rock cliffs slowly fracture stone as they grope toward water beneath the surface. All the while, planets orbit around the bright, weighty object of their focus.

Mistakenly we think of attention as gentle, even passive. In truth, it carries the force of desire, the gravity of survival and the heartbeat of formation.

Sociologist Robert N. Bellah wrote that attention is "how we use our psychic energy, and how we use our psychic energy determines the kind of self we are cultivating, the kind of person we are learning to be."[20] Christians are called to direct that attentive energy to the One who is the Bread of Life, the Living Water, the Word that was in the beginning with God. More than an attentional practice, this is soul cultivation.

For example, communal monastic chanting of the Psalms each

day is a Christian prayer practice that fosters mindfulness. It rests in a larger relational tradition and discipline extending into Christianity from Judaism, described in Scripture and possibly influenced by the Stoic practice of "continual reading" of precepts and other texts.[21] The praying person enters the silence, pays attention to what's on his or her mind and heart, and then directs attention to God, aided by the text and the community. When attention moves away from prayer and into the mind's preoccupations, the person notices that and shifts attention back to God. Even when one is praying the Psalms in solitude, the text and the practice create an awareness of the community of faith.

Christian mindfulness is informed and supported by texts, communities, tradition, teachers and guides, and the all-surrounding presence of God. In short, it is a spiritual discipline.

Spiritual disciplines have to do with how, and to what and whom, the mind is directed. Disciplines help people focus and shape their attention toward God and others with love and honesty, and they rest in traditions that support them. Not only about cultivating a sense of well-being, disciplines have devotional, moral and relational significance. The health they engender extends far beyond personal experiences of peace and happiness.

According to Peter Ochs, a professor of modern Judaic studies, Jewish morning prayer is the enacting of "a traditional and scripturally grounded ritual" in which the person who prays, though alone, is not solitary. The person at prayer is an agent of God, the "Creator and Guide," who is identified through the traditions of the people of faith: "Even alone, I do not make judgments and act alone but as participant in a greater community of judgment and action."[22] Awareness of community shapes attention in prayer and in life.

Praying with Scripture connects us with God and with what Christians call the "communion of saints"—persons of faith around the globe and throughout history. The devotional and communal connections may alleviate stress, but they don't pacify. On the contrary, as Ochs wrote, they inform both judgment and action.

A student of mine noted in a reflection paper that many children's "praise songs are written with words directly from the Bible," and simple bodily motions are often paired with the words. "These praises become prayers for me while we sing and move, and I learn about God's truth and God." Worshiping with the community, she prays with Scripture, taking in its assurance of love and also its truth. The songs become embodied in her and can surface later, even when she's alone. When that happens, she's moved back into prayer. The words, music and movements focus her attention on the Holy Spirit for whom her singing body is a temple. Singing Scripture cultivates mindful, whole-bodied prayer that is embedded in God, community and tradition.

Ochs writes that there is "an elemental three-ness in Morning Prayer: we, I, and the I of God."[23] The person, the community throughout history and around the globe, and God are all present in this practice. Spiritual disciplines forge robust links with the past and the future. Gratitude, correction and hope are cultivated through these disciplines, as the gravity of attention to God in the present moment allows the past and future to assume their proper orbits.

Contemporary secular attentional practices—mindfulness being most notable—contain movements of intention, attention and redirection of attention that are similar to the Judeo-Christian spiritual disciplines. The self-directing aspect of the person forms an intention and acts on it, notices the effect and then chooses to maintain or shift focus. We can see the immediate benefits of this, as so much of what's on our mind has to do with our concerns and doing something about them. A *spiritual* attentional practice offers more; it brings awareness into the sphere of love.

ATTENTION IN THE GOSPEL

The way love undergirds and shapes attention is evident in the account of Jesus' first visit to the home of Lazarus and his sisters Martha and Mary in Bethany (Luke 10:38-42). Martha served the meal and then complained to Jesus that she was doing all the work while Mary sat at his feet listening to him. Serving at the table was women's work. Mary's behavior of sitting at Jesus' feet and listening to him was countercultural.

Jesus drew Martha's attention to what was occupying her mind: "Martha, Martha, you are worried and distracted by many things" (v. 41). He then invited her to release those thoughts, freeing her to follow the deeper desires of her heart.

Perhaps Martha engaged in a mindfulness practice, noticing the mental and cultural impediments thwarting her desire as well as the feelings of envy stirred by her sister. Even positive disciplines of hospitality interfered with Martha's ability to sit at Jesus' feet and listen. Releasing her sense of duty in order to open her heart and mind to contemplative attention required an intentional, countercultural act.

Martha's story is so often our story. We neglect attentive disciplines because we're busy doing good things for our work, family, church and world. Just as Martha went about her tasks while Jesus was in her home, we too often become dehydrated even while our roots lie near streams of water. Training attention toward what's on one's mind and in one's heart is regarded by some as self-indulgent. Others find it too demanding. But it was just such a practice that Jesus validated in Bethany and elsewhere. Time after time, Jesus stopped and attended. He noticed what was on his mind and heart and helped others do the same.

Jon Kabat-Zinn often begins a mindfulness time by inviting those with him to sit and then "drop in." Mary sat and dropped into a space of quiet receptivity. She contemplated her Lord. Martha longed to do the same.

For Reflection

1. Consider your own ability to focus your attention. Describe the experience of being attentive.

2. Reflect on the practice of mindfulness and how Jesus helped Martha notice what was on her mind. Are there spiritual practices you engage in that help you notice what's on your mind? How do you move from mindfulness to prayer?

3. What have you noticed as the fruit cultivated in your life by attending to God?

7

Praying with Scripture

Your word is a lamp to my feet
and a light to my path.

Psalm 119:105

Long before today's attentional crisis, a number of religious traditions recommended the practice of praying with Scripture as a means of cultivating attention. Services in many Christian churches invite worshipers to be in prayer as Scripture is read, and many people also engage in the practice in solitude. When prayerful time and space is provided, mindful attention happens in the context of holy communication.

A Psalm a Day

During the last years of her life, my mother read a psalm every morning. In doing so she turned her attention to God and at times experienced God's attention turned toward her. Mom was a lifelong reader but began the daily practice of reading the Psalms only when she was in her eighties, drawn to it as she faced what she called her "last big adventure."

The Psalter's poetic prayers matched my mother's sense of life's paradoxes. Unlike some people, she had no problem with the psalmist's railing against God one minute and radiating adoration the next. Nearing ninety and spending her days in a wheelchair, she, too, alternated between feeling that God had forsaken her and, a moment later, knowing surely that she was watched over by a Good Shepherd.

Often during our daily phone conversations Mom mentioned the psalm she had read in the morning. I would imagine her bowing her white head over the page as she used her magnifying glass to read the words, then closing her eyes to absorb the message. She told me, "There's a lot of talk about enemies in the Psalms. I don't have enemies out to kill me the way David did, but I have plenty of enemies in my own head and body serving up discouragement and pain and making me feel defeated. Funny to think that makes me identify with a king!" She was comforted by reading that the Good Shepherd prepares a table for her in the midst of her enemies and anoints her head with oil.

As my mother read King David's complaints about enemies, she was helped to express her own laments about afflictions. Encountering his honesty in the midst of her morning prayer brought her feelings out into the open before God. Before doing so, she was simply held in the grip of the "enemies." Attention to her experience in the larger environment of God's grace released her from the tyranny of the experience.

Reading the Psalms each morning placed my mother's mortality within a graced awareness of God and of all the faithful people who had preceded her on earth. Her life wasn't diminished by the context; rather, it was uplifted, and her spirits with it. In the large space of God's presence, that dear woman beheld her worries, physical afflictions and responsibilities in the context of her belovedness.

Like my mother, I am a devotee of morning psalm reading. As my desire for quiet grew in midlife, I became acquainted with monastic life, and in the early 1990s I visited St. John's Abbey, a large Benedictine monastery in Minnesota. There I drank in the rich harmonies of monks chanting Scripture in the starkly modern church. Worshiping multiple times a day with monks, one is immersed in *lectio divina* (holy reading), especially of the Psalms.

LECTIO DIVINA

Lectio divina takes many forms. It usually involves reading or remembering words, but it can also be auditory or pictorial. When I lead people in this form of prayer, I read the verses aloud while they receive what they hear in prayer. People also pray with images. Stained-glass windows in medieval churches were a kind of "Bible of the poor," allowing people who could not read or did not have access to Bibles to see Scripture stories and pray with them.[1]

Many who write about the ancient monastic practice of praying with Scripture recommend four movements:

- *lectio* (reading the passage, noticing words and phrases that catch one's attention)
- *meditatio* (reading the passage again and meditating on it)
- *oratio* (reading the passage a third and final time and responding with prayer)
- *contemplatio* (wordlessly savoring the experience with God)[2]

Ordering the time of praying with Scripture according to these movements holds the focus, allowing the sacred words to become absorbed and metabolized. As with all attentional practices, we direct and redirect our attention.

Singing Scripture can also focus attention, allowing words to be taken deeply into ourselves as they play in our breath, on our lips and through our bodies. In *Cloister Walk,* her incandescent book about living with the monks of St. John's Abbey, Kathleen Norris wrote that as "a book of praises, meant to be sung, the Psalter contains a hope that 'human interest' stories tacked on to the end of a news broadcast cannot provide." My mother breakfasted on hope.

Norris continued: "The psalms mirror our world but do not allow us to become voyeurs. In a nation unwilling to look at its own violence, they force us to recognize our part in it. They make us reexamine our values."[3] The psalms spoke hope into my mother's world as she aged and as our country launched into twenty-first-century wars that troubled her. Psalm reading ushers worldly realities into the realm of prayer.

People throughout the millennia have found daily sustenance in Scripture. Guigo the Carthusian in the twelfth century,[4] reflecting on the words of Jesus' Sermon on the Mount, wrote, "As I read I hear the words: 'Blessed are the pure in heart, for they shall see God.' Here is a short text of Scripture, but one filled with a host of meanings, brimful of sweetness to nourish the soul. It is offered to us like a bunch of grapes."[5] We are what we eat, and holy writing is there to be ingested.

COMMUNAL LECTIO DIVINA

Tasting the words of life nourished me too, and, like Kathleen Norris, I was drawn to establish fellowship with a monastic order that chanted the Psalms. Growing up in the Episcopal Church, I had been imprinted with an appreciation for the vertical in worship: spires, acolytes extending lighted wands to tall altar tapers, vaulted ceilings, incense rising and the soaring notes of organ and chant. And Scripture was read at an elevated lectern, so the words flowed down over our bowed heads as we received it. The verticality of worship impressed on me the fact that though part of the congregation, I also stood in my own particular sightline to the Holy, which might just be somewhere above us. Monastic worship revived that experience for me at a time when my spiritual life had been greatly enriched by Protestant preaching and study of Scripture. I returned to Scripture as prayer, informed by years of knowing Scripture as teaching.

My appetite for contemplative prayer having been whetted by the Benedictine monks in Minnesota, I became a lay member or "oblate" (from the Latin word for offering) of the Camaldolese Benedictines, a small order of monks who combine the practices of monastic and eremitic (hermit) life. Their motherhouse in the United States is on the craggy Big Sur coastline a few hours from my home, off the grid and not far from considerably more costly opportunities for golden silence.

The first time I drove the long, curving road up to the hermitage, I felt I was returning more than arriving. New Camaldoli seemed like my soul's home, and on that first day I decided I wanted to make official the familial connection I felt with the persistently prayerful community perched over the ocean. A year or so after that first visit, having prayed every day as though I were with the monks, I returned with my husband and closest friend to be formally accepted as an oblate. The solemnity of my girlhood Episcopal confirmation ceremony was on my mind as I again responded to God's beckoning grace.

The Rule of the Camaldolese order comes from its medieval founder St. Romuald (who lived in Italy between 951 and 1027) and for centuries has been observed as a guideline for daily living by monks and oblates alike. The Brief Rule reads as follows:

> Sit in your cell as in paradise. Put the whole world behind you and forget it. Watch your thoughts like a good fisherman

watching for fish. The path you must follow is in the Psalms—
never leave it.

If you have just come to the monastery, and in spite of your
good will you cannot accomplish what you want, take every
opportunity you can to sing the Psalms in your heart and to
understand them with your mind.

And if your mind wanders as you read, do not give up; hurry
back and apply your mind to the words once more.

Realize above all that you are in God's presence, and stand
there with the attitude of one who stands before the emperor.

Empty yourself completely and sit waiting, content with the
grace of God, like the chick who tastes nothing and eats
nothing but what his mother brings him.[6]

This is a rule of contemplation aided by praying with Scripture.

As my relationship with the monks of New Camaldoli began, so
too did my daily sojourn with the Psalms. Every morning now as I
read the ancient words silently to myself in the darkness before dawn,
I imagine the voices of monks I have known in various places—on
the midwestern plains at St. John's, on the bluff at New Camaldoli
and at St. Catherine's Monastery in the Sinai Desert. I know that all
these brothers chant psalms every day without exception, as do communities of religious sisters and lay monastics around the world.
With them I visualize my mother reading a psalm and savoring the
communion she called "solitary splendor." As in the church of my
childhood, I feel part of a community while my bespoke soul com-
munes with the Holy One who watches over us all.

Praying with Scripture, as is clear in the Camaldolese Rule, is an
example of a Christian attentional practice. Mindfulness takes place,

as well as holy reading with prayerful attention to God. There is the intention to notice the mind's content (as a fisherman notices fish), the return of attention to a focal text (the Psalms) and the acceptance of what is experienced. What distinguishes this Christian practice from today's mindfulness movement is the distinctly theological context.

A student who engaged in lectio divina for a course I taught about prayer wrote, "In those times of silence, I have felt the infinity of God's majesty, glory, and love for me as a closer reality, and this has brought an increased sense of peace in my life." Attention to Scripture places her life and world within the remembered reality of God's grace. And she is changed.

SPIRITUAL CULTIVATION THROUGH PRAYING WITH SCRIPTURE: AN ILLUSTRATION

As an assignment for a course about Christian spiritual disciplines that I've taught for New College Berkeley, Regent College (in Vancouver) and Fuller Theological Seminary, I ask students to choose a post-resurrection story from the Gospels and pray with it every day for a month. Doing so establishes the discipline of praying God's Word.

The practice focuses the student on the postresurrection period in the disciples' lives, which holds so many parallels to our lives of faith. Like Jesus' contemporaries grieving his recent death, we, too, desire God, we sometimes experience God and, when the experience dims, we return to desiring, seeking and grasping for God.

Many students spend a month with the Road to Emmaus story found in Luke 24. What follows is an example of a student's journal entries during his month-long lectio divina experience with this passage of Scripture.

> Day 1: Dear Lord: As I read I try to imagine myself as one of the disciples, walking to Emmaus. What would it have been

like to have just experienced the crucifixion of Christ earlier in the week, and three days later, hear about his missing body? . . . How many times have I been like these disciples: so consumed by the events of my life that I have failed to notice Jesus in my circumstances? What would it be like to be aware of Jesus in my life "24-7"? How would it change the quality of my life? I can't even imagine it.

The student tried to imagine the experience of the people on the Emmaus road as they fled Jerusalem. They were "consumed by events" in a world that had taken on circuslike qualities. Jesus, the man they loved as Lord and friend, had been brutally killed. Many of his followers, their companions, were dispersed and in danger. The world was violent and mean, and they were getting away from it. Their experience shed light on the student's own attempts to recognize the presence of the Holy One. He read the text of his life by the light of the Word: *lectio.*

As he prayed, his experience deepened:

Day 2: Dear Lord: I am like Cleopas. I get stuck "discussing" the events of my days, too. I get so distracted by what has happened in my life that I turn my focus away from [You]. I drift. . . . I can almost hear the Holy Spirit warning me to be careful: the sanctification process is easily stymied by an undisciplined thought life.

What's evident even by the second day of praying with Scripture is the praying person's growth in self-awareness through mindfulness. He noticed that he was distracted. Attending to God alerted him to what God might be saying, and the message received was one of correction and invitation. Through discipline he received the relational experience he wanted.

He read that Jesus came to the people on the road and asked them what they were talking about as they walked along. Jesus attended to them with interest. Then, hearing the confused mix of their thoughts and feelings (indications of the trauma they had suffered), he opened the words of Scripture to them. The student received words of Scripture, too, in the midst of the fullness of his own life. Not only reading and meditating on his experience, he joined God in God's Word.

> Day 10: Dear Lord: I find myself stuck on your initial question to the disciples: "What are you discussing together as you walk along?" (Luke 24:27). Each time I run it through my mind, I find the Holy Spirit revealing a different facet of insight. It's like stepping back from my life a bit and gaining your perspective on things, regarding whatever happens to be going on at the time. It's a way of being more aware of your presence in my life! What a great way to check in and restore my spiritual equilibrium.

This is a description of how healthy attention and attachment are seamlessly joined in the spiritual discipline of praying with Scripture. Jesus' question to the two people on the road became the question this man returned to as a living question for his own life. As Scripture says, "The word of God is living and powerful, and sharper than any two-edged sword, piercing even to the division of soul and spirit, and of joints and marrow, and is a discerner of the thoughts and intents of the heart" (Hebrews 4:12 NKJV). The student pondered God's Word day after day, seeing more in himself as the words sank into him: *meditatio.*

The living Spirit engaged the student in holy reflection on the road he was walking that semester. His recognition that it was the One who is Love posing the question enabled him to look honestly at things in himself he might not want to see. The love allowed insight, and insight amplified love.

> Day 11: Dear Lord: When I brought the experience of the Road to Emmaus into my day yesterday, my eyes were opened for a time (Luke 24:31). [He writes about being in a public place where he would have ordinarily been irritated by the presence of others. Instead he remembered how Jesus was with the people on the Emmaus road. Then, rather than being frustrated by strangers in a public place, he found himself interested in them.] . . . How everything changes when I deliberately imagine you there with me in my day. It's not just about coming into your presence when I pray with others, have my quiet time or attend . . . classes. Life is not secular and sacred. . . . It is scary and exciting all at the same time.

Grace suffused his life.

The Emmaus road walkers invited Jesus to their table, and he broke the bread and blessed it. Even though Jesus then vanished from their sight, everything was changed after they had been in his loving, sight-restoring presence. Hope fortified, they "at once" returned to Jerusalem, seemingly no longer wary of strangers on the open road. The praying student found that imagining Jesus with him through daily lectio divina with the Emmaus road story transformed his experience of strangers. He registered their presence with Jesus' eyes, and doing so prompted more compassion than he would normally have felt.

The student was practicing a spiritual discipline. Praying with the passage wasn't just a task checked off a to-do list, nor was it an empty habit that became reflexive. It engaged his self and diminished his selfishness. He spoke to God the words that the Word evoked in him: *oratio*.

As time went by, the student's relationship with God went through different emotional terrain, which points to the vitality of this practice. Sometimes he felt discontentment and asked God to stay close to him in that. His attention wandered and doubts arose. Praying with Scripture engaged the kind of metacognitive processes people seek in meditative practices as well as in spiritual direction; specifically, the processes of heightened awareness (he noticed his experience) and disidentification (he noticed that he is more than his thoughts and feelings). Intentionally and receptively, he noticed what was going on in his own awareness and kept returning his attention to God.

Like Jews and Christians engaged in morning prayer, the praying student was receptively attentive to and aware of present events and experience. His undefended consciousness of his mind, which included hopes, fears, distractions and renewed concentration, was enhanced by prayer. Though solitary, it was a deeply relational practice. He noticed what God was showing him and what he was asking of God. There was satisfaction, but not always peace and ease. He felt corrected by a loving God and he confessed, allowing his will and actions to be molded by God's grace. Compassion grew, stretching his heart. In God-oriented attentional practice, the devotional and the diaconal—prayer and loving service—entwine.

Day 20: Dear Lord: "Being" is not to be mistaken for passivity. I am not to stay at the table with you, but to get up and walk, too. . . . Thank you for the gift of table fellowship.

In the midst of doubts and temptations to leave both road and table, the student kept returning to a posture of receptivity. Having received, he wanted the grace to flow through him to others as it did with the people at Emmaus. Awe and compassion went hand in hand as his hunger was satisfied with the One who is the Bread of Life. The Word was digested and metabolized. Fortified, he continued his journey. He had experienced intimacy with God: *contemplatio.*

WATERING THE SOIL

In a month of praying with a Scripture passage and journaling, we see God cultivating the student's soul, time and again, through the movements of lectio divina. A study of preaching pastors in New Zealand found that praying with Scripture as a regular spiritual discipline was spiritually nourishing and restored for pastors a connection between devotion and the ministry of preaching.[7] As with the students I've taught, the relationship between receptivity and generativity is evident in the pastors' experience—the grace they receive flows to others.

The prophet Isaiah expressed it this way:

> For as the rain and the snow come down from heaven,
>   and do not return there until they have watered the earth,
> making it bring forth and sprout,
>   giving seed to the sower and bread to the eater,
> so shall my word be that goes out from my mouth;
>   it shall not return to me empty
> but it shall accomplish that which I purpose,
>   and succeed in the thing for which I sent it. (Isaiah 55:10-11)

Like rain and snow to the earth, God's Word enters lives, cultivating the person and changing the world. We become well-watered pilgrims, walking trees.

What is cultivated is radically different from what our media cultivate in us. We are not mere spectators or performers; rather, we are active participants in God's world. This is also radically different from "sitting alone" with our thoughts, which researchers have been finding is uncomfortable for most people; in fact, sitting and doing nothing for a few minutes is so unpleasant that some research subjects, given the opportunity, prefer to press a button that gives them a mild electric shock![8]

While lectio divina often involves sitting and doing nothing, we are not sitting alone. God is present and wants to know about our lives. *What's on your mind and heart as you walk through your days?* the Word asks. *What things?*

For Reflection

1. There are secular and sacred attentional practices, and you may already engage in some regularly. What helps you maintain those practices? What interferes?

2. As a contemplative prayer practice, lectio divina requires us to enter into silence and awareness before we turn toward God's Word. Some people find silence uncomfortable. What helps you be in silence (possibly short intervals; the company of others; solitude . . .)?

3. Pay attention to the words that draw you toward prayer. Perhaps you have a daily practice of reading Scripture. If so, allow yourself to pause and metabolize any word or phrase that catches your attention.

CULTIVATING ATTACHMENT

Whoever does not love does not know God, for God is love.

1 JOHN 4:8

*T*HE HEART'S CRIES ARE RELATIONAL: "Help me!" "Thank you!" "Why?" We call out to someone, even if we have no idea who that someone might be. Our hearts open as we cry and, being open, are able to receive. Christian Scripture asserts that the One to whom we cry responds to us with love. It's a heart-to-heart relationship. Has that been your experience? Have you, like King David, cried "How long, O LORD?" (Psalm 13:1) and then discovered, after pouring out your heart, that you've received a hint of Love's presence? My guess is that you wouldn't be reading this book unless the answer to that question is *yes*, however tentative and qualified.

Like any relationship, ours with God requires effort, and a spirituality of cultivation calls for discipline, not for the sake of duty or perfection but for the sake of thriving. Countering strong forces in our culture, spiritual disciplines increase our capacity to choose ordered attention and attachment. Attention helps us notice what's real, while attachment connects us to all that matters—including people, places, ideas and the Holy. It's a circular truth: attention (for instance, noticing hints of grace) begets attachment (love), which aids attention (knowing God, the other and ourselves better), and the spiral continues.

Rooted Freedom and Its Absence

The word *discipline* sounds severe. Time and effort must be invested in a discipline. It's work that requires us to say no to invitations and inclinations. But we're called to freedom! Paul understood the compound truth of being constrained yet free: "For freedom Christ has set us free" (Galatians 5:1), and, also through Christ, we are "being rooted and grounded in love" (Ephesians 3:17). Free and rooted. Walking trees. Disciplines root us in the love that gives us life and freedom, just as the steady deepening of a tree's roots toward water secures it so its branches may sway freely in the wind.

Abraham Joshua Heschel described the poles of prayer as regularity or structure (*keva*) and the spontaneity of our hearts (*kavanah*). Equilibrium is achieved when they are held in equal force. The *keva* of prayer practice is subject to our control, but Heschel, quoting the medieval rabbi and physician Moses Maimonides, asserts that "prayer without kavanah is no prayer at all."[1] The act without the love is meaningless, possibly what Paul calls a clanging cymbal (1 Corinthians 13:1).

God desires relationship with us—full stop. Disciplines hold space in which our desire for God can be kindled and in which we just might notice God. Just as the body gives the spirit (or breath) a place in which to do its life-giving work, so the regularity of a discipline holds a place in which our spontaneous response to God might happen. The structure cradles the life force, just as rootedness allows for responsiveness.

Within our circuslike culture, spiritual disciplines can be easily abandoned as our days divide between stressful work and disengaged pastimes, neither offering the nourishment that walking trees require. Such a life leaves us inattentive and even detached from ourselves, others and the Holy. As noted earlier, disorders of attention and attachment are now treated in adults as well as children, while many more people suffer from conditions of fragmented attention and undernourished relationships that don't warrant diagnosis or clinical treatment.

A recent public story illustrates a level of disordered attention and attachment not uncommon today. The context is that in the *Atlantic* in 2012, a reporter posted data about federally paid annual leave and holiday times for twenty-one advanced economies (member countries of the Organisation for Economic Development and Co-operation). Among these countries, the United States is the only one that does not offer federally guaranteed paid days away from work; however, many US companies do offer vacation time, which many employees do not fully take.

By the end of 2011, 57 percent of American workers had accumulated up to two weeks of unused annual vacation time. Readers wrote to the article's author to explain why this is so, and their responses reflect our culture's circus polarity. Given that I was thinking about disordered attention and attachment when I read the story, I was especially intrigued by what one person wrote:

> I have too much vacation and don't take it. And when I do I end up working or doing the equivalent of work anyway. Cause I don't have anything else to do. Or extra money to go anywhere and do anything. And "staycations" are a joke. I just end up sleeping, watching TV and . . . working. Cause I just get bored. It also takes as much time and money and effort

to get anywhere as it does to actually be there and enjoy it so what's the point? Plus I'd have to go by myself anyway and while I'm okay with that, most things aren't really amenable to it. I dunno, my identity is wrapped up in my work and I'm happier when I work. If I'm not working then I get restless and I can think about the things I don't like about my life. It may not be healthy but it is what it is at this point.[2]

This lament sounds like a contemporary version of Ecclesiastes: All is pointless and wearisome. Work is endless, relationships empty. The sun rises, the sun sets. Nothing is new under the sun, and there is no health in us.

Constant work punctuated by empty vegetative activity has yielded a woeful absence of sustained, meaningful attention and attachment. This respondent to the *Atlantic* article alternates between working long hours and vegging out in boring ways and, to make it worse, has no significant companion with whom to get away from it all or, presumably, to share the daily misery.

There's also the hint that getting off the work treadmill might allow for an unsettling awareness: "If I'm not working then I get restless and I can think about the things I don't like about my life." Without times of deeper reflective attention, some of it uncomfortable, personal transformation is impossible, and so is the kind of reflection that prompts social change and correction. Such reflection requires going beneath the voice of resignation that sighs, "It is what it is." This ceaselessly working person might benefit from a companion who cares to listen.

Inescapable demands of the workplace and unrestricted electronic accessibility can disrupt attention and the cultivation of attachments. Attention and attachment are also impeded by the kinds of relaxation facilitated by our culture's menu of alcohol and other mood-altering substances, overeating, surfing television channels and the Internet, vicariously living through celebrities and pundits in the media, roaming shopping malls, and other vitality-dissipating activities that permit us to step out of life's frenetic pace.

While contemporary conditions prompt us toward disengagement, that possibility is present in all kinds of cultures. The state of uncaring listlessness was called *acedia* by fourth-century desert father John Cassian, who described a monk as follows: "He looks about anxiously this way and that, and sighs that none of the brethren come to see him, and often goes in and out of his cell, and frequently gazes up at the sun, as if it was too slow in setting, and so a kind of unreasonable confusion of mind takes possession of him like some foul darkness."[3] The listless, disengaged pole of circus living is just as unsatisfying as the frenetic one, and the twenty-first-century worker bored by "staycations" and the sighing monk suffer in similar ways.

We will all experience seasons of such suffering, but there are helpful tools at hand in the form of spiritual practices. By countering the circus forces of under- and overactivation, which threaten to fragment our attention and fracture attachments, these disciplines offer structures in which our hearts may quicken.

ATTACHMENT AND ITS DISCONTENTS

Having lifelines of attachment in place is crucial and requires maintenance. My mother had a few soul friends with whom she spoke almost every day, and it was my privilege to be one of them. Sometimes the conversations were light and cheerful, and at other times they plunged to the depths of grief. Our daily conversations weren't always easy for me, logistically or emotionally, but they were infusions of love and grace.

Perhaps it has never been easy for people to take time in their day and make room in their hearts for what matters most. But with increasingly little time spent in reflective practices and greater investment in all kinds of screen time, we know ourselves less well and have a decreasing capacity for empathy.[4]

With attention disorders, as noted, the clinical diagnosis contains two contrasting dominant types, an inattentive subtype and a hyperactive, impulsive subtype. Similarly, the primary types of attachment disorders are the inhibited-attachment avoidant form and the disinhibited-anxious attachment variety. A 2010 estimate of the state of attachment among American adults was that while most people are securely attached, 25 percent are avoidant of attachments, and 20 percent have an anxious attachment style.[5] Both are forms of suffering, in many cases the result of deprivation and loss in childhood.

As with attention disorders, these types of attachment disorders are mirrored among those of us without diagnoses and whose childhoods allowed for secure attachment, yet whose days too often alternate between vegetative and frenzied extremes. As you read about these two categories of attachment disorders, you can probably think of individuals who fit the descriptions. Some people are acutely withdrawn and detached from almost everyone. It's been claimed that the Silicon Valley technology boom relied on the tireless work of such types, and Peter Thiel, an early Facebook investor, claims that the people who run Internet firms "are sort of autistic."[6] People at this end of the attachment disorder pole, even without a clinical diagnosis and sometimes with great professional success, often suffer from isolation and loneliness.

Indeed, social scientists are finding that loneliness rates are soaring in the American population overall. In the year 2000, 20 percent of Americans over forty-five years of age said they were chronically lonely, a statistic that grew to more than 30 percent a decade later.[7]

At the other extreme of the attachment disorder spectrum are the anxiously attached. These people are excessively eager to engage with almost anyone, or they become overly attached to a particular person or persons. Many psychotherapists have written about the problem of codependency, which, though variously defined, has to do with unhealthy attachments of this kind. The behaviors of anxiously attached persons may be shaped by fears of loneliness, and while social media may ease the experience of isolation, the shallowness of the connections can also exacerbate it.

WORK-BASED ATTACHMENTS

Work has pride of place on most of our calendars, as Genesis tells us it did in God's week too. Work is significant and is part of what we were made for, though in the situations of many people around the world, social change is needed to bring about economic and employment justice. For many of the people reading this book, what's needed is discernment about the growing hours of the workweek and about the psychological and spiritual problem that develops when work determines our identity, becomes the gravitational center of life and is the locus of most of our relationships. Even when a person experiences work as a kind of home and co-workers as family, it is fundamentally a place where attachment is governed by economic exigencies. The workplace is not a place of unencumbered or secure relating.

Working near California's Silicon Valley, psychologist and sociologist Ilene Philipson studied the effects of a work-home inversion in people's lives. She claims that for many of her psychotherapeutic clients, work—not home—is their "life" and what gives them purpose. Philipson wrote,

> The new work order—spearheaded by the high-tech companies
> of Silicon Valley—is creating total company cultures that offer

engagement, a shared sense of purpose, exhilaration, and interpersonal connection that is increasingly absent in people's families and communities outside the workplace. As divorce, geographic mobility, social fragmentation and the decline of
neighborhood, community and civic participation grow, more
and more of us are turning to the workplace for the satisfaction
of needs formerly filled by family, friends and neighbors.[8]

When their jobs come to an end, these corporate employees feel
lost, betrayed and "devastated, feeling as though they are aliens or
exiles from a society that increasingly values commitment to and
identification with work over all else."[9] Attachments that seemed
real and enduring ended with the loss of the job.

A few years after Philipson's analysis, the great recession of 2008
precipitated rising unemployment, underemployment, work-
related migration and moonlighting, all further eroding people's
ability to maintain attachments. Also, increasing numbers of
workers no longer work in shared places, telecommuting instead
from wherever they are in the world.

A SPIRITUAL AND DEVELOPMENTAL CYCLE

Research supports the commonsense understanding that being well
attended to by a parent when one is a child promotes more secure
attachments throughout life. Moreover, those who are more securely attached to others are more inclined and better able to offer
interpersonal attention.[10] Healthy attention, on the whole, fosters
healthy attachment, which in turn cultivates the capacity for attention—a developmental cycle that spiritual disciplines support.

The attention-attachment-attention cycle is a devotional reality
as well as a developmental one. This is good news, for we cannot
control the conditions into which we are born; we may not enter

the world in the company of attentive, loving adults who enable us to form secure attachments; work relationships may be severed; and calamity may shatter our capacities for attention and attachment. Even so, by the mystery of faith we may find ourselves able to turn toward the One who calls to us. By grace we may also discover others who are devoted to God and humankind and who extend welcome to us. And then with them we may tell stories and engage in practices that bring healing and rootedness to our lives. This is what communities of faith hope to cultivate.

The Christian spirituality literature has a long tradition of examining attachment, encouraging people to achieve a healthy detachment (or nonattachment) from unhealthy concerns (such as fear, worry, lust, pride, selfish promotion and ceaseless striving) and connections (including possessiveness, idolatry, tyranny and more). The tradition also offers relational disciplines for cultivating healthy, ordered attachments to God and others, bringing them into better alignment so that we love what and whom we ought to love with a freedom that neither grasps nor withholds.

We see this cultivation of attention and attachment in the stories of the Christian faith, including the Emmaus story. Jesus' attention to the traumatized people on the road enabled them to open their hearts to their own feelings, to him and to Scripture. Then joy sent them hastening down the road at night to share their good news with those they loved. I see this dynamic in people who pray. The love they receive flows through them into the world.

Attached to the One Who Is Love and Truth

The poet W. H. Auden wrote, "We must love one another or die,"[11] and this is exactly what scientists are finding. Ill people who are lonely tend to get sicker and die more quickly than those with the same disease who are not suffering from loneliness. People who place a high importance on religion and frequently attend worship services score higher on inventories of personal well-being.[12]

We are cultivated by the One who is Love. As I listen to people in spiritual direction, I witness how they participate with God in the cultivation of their souls. Recently a directee was coming to terms with a medical diagnosis that might mean he was nearing the end of his life far sooner than he'd anticipated. Initially anxiety and anger coursed through him, keeping him awake at night as his mind searched for solutions. Over time his wrestling became prayer, which lessened his anxiety and anger without draining energy from his efforts to avert early death.

During this time he visited relatives who lived at a distance. He told me that his experience of mortality shaped the visit: "I want to show up for others as who I really am. I'm feeling how much I want to stay connected with those I love. A large part of what I hope they'll remember after I'm gone is how I saw them, the good I recognize in them. That's what I try to communicate." Prayer seemed to cultivate greater love for himself and for those close to him. Love is his legacy.

As was the case for the bereft people on the Emmaus road, this man's circumstances remained difficult and not at all as he wished. Yet from the vantage of his connection to God, everything looked different. His difficulties no longer eclipsed everything else. Life flowed to and through him, even in the valley of the shadow of death. The lamenting writer of Ecclesiastes (5:1) encourages us to "draw near to listen" to God, and that's what this man did.

Scripture tells us that God is Truth as well as Love. Love "rejoices in the truth" (1 Corinthians 13:6), and Jesus counsels us to be as wise as serpents in facing truth and as harmless as doves in acting from love (Matthew 10:16). The Holy One, who regards us with a long, loving look, directs our attention to what's real.

Conversely, the self-help culture has repackaged and promoted the proverbial wisdom that happiness and success are within our control—and therefore failure and pain are our own fault. If you suffer from heart disease, you probably have erred in letting yourself be a Type A person, ceaselessly striving to achieve. If you suffer from cancer, perhaps you exposed yourself to the wrong chemicals or didn't ingest the right ones. If you die, maybe you didn't fight valiantly enough for your life. Partial truths, conveyed coldly, add insult to injury.

Barbara Ehrenreich warns against the dangers of "bright-siding," assigning inordinate power to positive thinking. Doing so creates the illusion of control, depletes compassion for those who suffer and erodes efforts to correct personal and social problems. Bright-siding is part of an environment of can-do thinking that makes no concession to mortal processes beyond our control.

The church, too, can fall prey to the culture of positive illusion. Ehrenreich writes,

> The seeker who embraces positive theology finds him- or herself in a seamless, self-enclosed world, stretching from workplace to mall to corporate-style church. Everywhere, he or she hears the same message—that you can have all that stuff in the mall, as well as the beautiful house and car, if only you believe that you can. But always, in a hissed undertone, there is the darker message that if you don't have all that you want, if you feel sick, discouraged, defeated, you have only yourself to blame. Positive theology ratifies and completes a world without beauty, transcendence, or mercy.[13]

Absorbing presentations of reality inconsistent with God's truth and love impede our growth. Spiritual disciplines attune and re-attune us to the One who is truth in love, and in so doing cultivate compassion and moral response. They open the flow from attachment to attention to attachment. History testifies to this with the lives of those who pray with Scripture. It's what I hear in spiritual direction.

FACING TRUTH IN THE COMPANY OF LOVE:
AN ILLUSTRATION

A few years ago I had the privilege of accompanying a directee as she faced hard truths in her life. I'd been seeing Ellen for a year, and our times together took place between her long days in the corporate world and long evenings with her husband and teenage children. One time she arrived especially exhausted, dressed in a business suit, and wearing running shoes for after-work comfort. I lit the candle and said, "We light the candle as a reminder that God is with us." She smiled, watched the flame take hold, sighed, closed her eyes and began to breathe slowly and deeply.

Ellen told me she'd had a great vacation and had been back at work for a few days. She spoke about work dissatisfactions and being tired, too tired to engage in activities she enjoyed.

Rumi writes, "Close both eyes to see with the other eye."[14] Asking God to give me an eye to what was true, I attuned to what seemed at play beneath Ellen's surface story. We began an exploration of different parts of the narrative, testing for energy and depth, noticing what held weight or shifted. I hoped to offer Ellen what Freud called an "evenly hovering attention,"[15] an openhanded engagement that would help her move toward what God (my word, not Freud's) would have her see.

Suddenly she looked at me with shock, her eyes and mouth forming a triangle of Os. I didn't know what we'd come upon, but I knew that something unconscious had emerged into consciousness, like an iceberg surfacing. I felt my heart reach toward her and may even have leaned toward her physically. I experienced

awe in all its dimensions: a heightened state of full and total observation, a diminished awareness of myself and complete focus on
Ellen's experience. I was riveted.

Ellen told me about a conversation she'd had with her husband
ten days earlier while on vacation. He had revealed something to
her, a possible intention, direction and decision in his life. If taken,
it would overturn her life, at least for the time being. Apparently
she had repressed all memory of the conversation, not even remembering it a few days later when she had seen her therapist.
Submerged, lurking below her conscious awareness, it had drained
her of life and energy.

Ellen's energy returned with the memory, and she moved from
sobbing to laughing, catastrophizing to minimizing. I tried to
hold the whole truth: the magnitude of the situation, the love and
hope she had for her husband and their lives, the self-protective
way her mind had not remembered, and her faith in a loving God
with her in it all.

She looked at the flickering candle flame, robust and responsive.
The wax was fully melted and clear, just as Ellen's view into her own
depths had become. Sounding a bit like Julian of Norwich, who
said, "All shall be well, and all shall be well, and all manner of thing
shall be well,"[16] Ellen concluded our time saying, "No matter what
happens, all will turn out well because God will get me through
this, even though it might be a horrendous process."

After Ellen left, I went back into my office, which was smoky
with the extinguished flame. The candle wax was beginning to cool,
regaining its opacity and firmness, while the wastebasket held tear-
soaked tissues. I remained a while in what felt like a numinous
"thin place" between earth and heaven, metabolizing the gravity of
what I'd heard. Spiritual direction can assume the movements of
lectio divina: hearing the words, meditating on them, responding

and then resting in contemplation. As I sat with all I'd heard, I felt God near.

RELATIONSHIP DISCIPLINES

In addition to helping people become more attentive to the realities of humanness, faith in the One who is Truth and Love opens us to the realm of transcendent realities. Ellen's elusive truth was able to emerge in the holding environment of the larger Truth. Spiritual direction was a relational spiritual discipline that helped Ellen open her heart to God. In a time that seemed to threaten human attachments, attachment to God anchored her.

Reexperiencing that anchoring attachment to God in the context of the attachment she and I share, Ellen was able to attend to what was real in her life. Doing so was painful. Belden Lane writes that the "practice of paying attention is the rarest of gifts because it depends upon the harshest of disciplines."[17] Some of these disciplines—like listening, sabbath keeping, lectio divina and spiritual direction—are practices that much of our culture ignores, mocks or blocks. Their difficulty is ameliorated by love. For while attention is essential to cultivation, it is motivated and sustained by our attachments. As we love and are loved by God, we are strengthened in our ability to pay attention.

Just as our bodies require maintenance, so do our relationships, yet as persons and communities of faith we have sorely neglected our rich Christian tradition of spiritual practices. Recent Barna research has found that only 52 percent of Christians in the United States are making efforts—exerting discipline—to grow spiritually, and "many of these are inconsistent and achieve limited results."[18] Our lives, churches and culture are poorer as a result.

Our relationships with God and people require practices. Peter Ogle, my blogging acquaintance who died in his late fifties, was part of the 52 percent of American Christians who do make an effort to grow spiritually. He prayed, "Make me wholly yours. I am your apprentice, and I stand at your crucible of life, wiping the sweat and grit from my furrowed brow."[19] Spiritual discipline is relational work.

As a modern Ecclesiastes might point out, we may not find satisfaction through all of our climbing, balancing, juggling, launching and scoring. We may not become part of the world's elite, be spared hard truths or live to a ripe old age. But every one of us may be cultivated, by God's grace, as we participate with Love in our becoming.

FOR REFLECTION

1. Consider your relationships. Write about one or two.

2. Which of your relationships involve a healthy attachment—neither detached nor overattached? What criteria are important to you in evaluating healthy attachments?

3. Consider a relationship that you care about and that's in need of attention. As you pray about it, what comes to mind as a way to foster a healthier relationship?

Spiritual Direction

A ship with a good navigator comes safely to port, God willing.

John Climacus

Throughout decades of joyful immersion in the practice of spiritual direction, I've become increasingly aware of how attention and attachment intertwine in the lives of those to whom I listen. Engaging in the discipline of spiritual direction is a way these people have chosen to cultivate their lives. As I began working on this book, I reflected on how spiritual direction has cultivated my soul, through practices of attention and attachment, both as a director and as a directee.

Accompanied by a Good Navigator

Following my parents' deaths, my attentive capacities were sorely attenuated. For the first few months, whenever I picked up a book I would read the same page over and over again, not absorbing much of anything. Some tasks I was able to do from my rational mind—such as the administrative tasks of putting my parents' affairs in order—but, as with reading, I didn't absorb much.

During that time of new grief I was surprised to discover that muddled as I was, my heart was able to open to other people. Their stories engaged me; in fact, my empathic availability to the suffering of others seemed enhanced by my own suffering. It was as though the other person and I both stood by the shore at low tide, beholding depths usually hidden. Relating to another person's heart enabled my own to pay attention.

What I couldn't do was anything that required the cooperation of my analytical mind with my heart. Expository writing was out of the question for many months after my parents' deaths, which posed a problem given that this book was under contract. Every time I sat down to write, I veered into repetitive thoughts or just sat in front of the computer staring off into space as feelings swept over me. My mind or my heart might be engaged, but integrating the two seemed impossible as I grieved.

One day during that year I visited Jean Shinoda Bolen, a psychiatrist and analyst with whom I'd been consulting about my spiritual direction practice and who, for some months when I was between spiritual directors, served as my de facto director. A noted writer, Jean took an interest in how my writing was going and asked about my work on *The Cultivated Life*. I confessed that I'd been unable to write much of anything. I told her that there appeared to be a writer's block planted squarely between my reason and the rest of me. I'm sure I sighed.

Jean turned our conversation toward my grief. I tried to describe it: My mental image of where I was at the time was a stormy sea. Battered by shallow waves and also rolling currents that welled up toward me from the ocean's depths with dreadful force, I was simply trying to stay afloat. Both kinds of waves seemed relentless.

On the surface of my life, little reminders of my parents whipped my heart and sapped my energy. Harder to endure were the slow, deep waves of sadness that came from beneath my awareness. I registered their approach viscerally, with nausea and dread mounting, as if hearing the opening chords of the shark's music in *Jaws*. Those swells came from the edges of my awareness and, powerless to stave them off, I merely braced for the wallop.

The surface waves could be traversed relatively quickly. I would notice a needlepoint pillow my mother had given me, feel the pain of her love in her absence and then go about my day. Or I would receive a legal invoice related to my parents' deaths, again feel my grief, pay the bill and move on. But the deep waves had a long arc as they approached and passed.

My director listened to me, and I felt her care. She nodded, and I felt she understood. She assured me that the power of the waves would diminish but that it would take time.

What Direction Allows

As we sat together in that sheltering hour of our attention to my life, I began to notice the ocean in which I floated and in which all the wave action was taking place. Before I spoke of the ocean imagery to Jean, I had been oblivious to all but the waves. In her company it became apparent to me that I wasn't afraid of drowning. In fact, I felt assured that I would float and survive.

The reflective space of Jean's listening enabled me to see more of the picture. I was held by the imagery, but I was not alone in it. That eased my dread. The act of telling my story to someone who cared gave it shape. Together we were cultivating the story and, as we did, I brought into the light of awareness some elements that had been lurking within me. Grief was present, and I could regard it without being dominated by it.

My existence in the buoying, enveloping ocean was what I hadn't beheld on my own. I discovered that I was floating, upheld by a force more constant than the waves. I registered, too, my director's caring attention as a present echo of that larger holding. In the end my kind listener said, "I think the book might begin to flow if you allowed your parents into it." The thought of doing so had never crossed my mind. But when I opened my heart to her suggestion, the flow did begin as my heart and mind worked in concert.

While I was grieving I sought spiritual direction, and the regular, boundaried structure of that time enabled me to open what had been locked within me. The spiritual direction sessions formed a temple in which God's Spirit and my spirit could meet, even though my consultant's faith was different from my own. Like any skillful spiritual listener, she held the space and offered a loving and directive attention that helped me hear myself and listen for God. In paying attention to me as I grieved, Jean Bolen helped *me* pay attention. Attached to her through the practice of spiritual direction, I could experience my bereavement as though the connection with her held me on belay while I rappelled down into the grief. There, in it, I discovered the ocean that spoke to me of grace.

Friends and family accompanied me in my grief. They listened to me, sat with me and held me. They loved me, and many of them share my faith in Jesus Christ and prayed with and for me. But those relationships are mutual, so I also attended to the others' lives as best I could. Some of them are so close to me that my grief generated turbulent wave action for them.

Spiritual direction is a relational discipline in my life. I was grateful that it was in place when I needed someone standing outside my life to hear the sorrow in my heart and help me go deeper into the truth of it. It's an attentional practice in the context of a nonmutual relationship. I didn't learn about Jean's life. In our hour together, I had the freedom to stay with my own story, my own experience and sightings of God.

NAVIGATION AS AN AID TO CULTIVATION

Spiritual direction is a practice in which I've participated for a number of decades, and I've also been cultivated by God's grace through being a director.[1] A spiritual director is an undershepherd or undergardener to the Holy One who guides and nurtures. Accompanying other people on their journeys of faith sheds light on who that Holy One is, as well as on what is possible in a life of faith. I am inspired by the honesty and courage I witness in people who see me for direction, and I'm often flooded by what I see as an emanation of God's love for the person sitting in the blue chair in front of me. In a body familiar with the pathogens of stress, I've been grateful to so often be awash in the salutogens of grace.

For spiritual directees, telling our story to a listening person can provide reflective distance so that we're not simply engulfed by the driving narrative. We are able to enter the story completely enough to see its contours. Meaning becomes more apparent, as do categories of significance—what matters, what's most important, what goodness or truth is revealed by the story. Telling the story embeds it in memory, because in the telling of it our feelings are engaged. What we're saying literally runs through our bodies, not just off the tongue but through our neurotransmitters, through our endocrine system and possibly through tear ducts and the nerves responsible for galvanic skin response.

Prior to that meeting with Jean Bolen, I had been able to construct the discipline of writing this book—setting time aside, composing outlines, doing relevant research and preparing the writing space—but in order for my words to be authentic, they needed to be fed from wells of feeling, intuition and imagination, in addition to intellect. By forcing myself to write in a way that cut off my grief, I'd rendered myself root-bound. The tree that I am was in too small a container. No amount of surface pruning could counteract the stunting congestion beneath the surface. In order to flourish, I needed to be able to stretch the roots of my being to their full length.

In listening to me, my consultant and temporary director helped me replace the too-small container with a larger space in which the pain and densely rich truth from my unfurling "roots" could flow into my life and work. What she offered was a form of healing—a loving attachment—which freed me to attend to my life and the grace that was shaping it.

Having my story flow through all parts of myself as I spoke to Jean, I became more integrated. I was restored to greater wholeness,[2] and though I would remain bereft of my parents, I was no longer so fragmented by the loss. In the shelter of another person's attention and God's all-surrounding grace, telling my story rewove me.

THE DISCIPLINE OF SPIRITUAL DIRECTION

Spiritual direction is one among many disciplines devoted to God's cultivation of souls. It's also a formal art of accompanying people as they turn their attention toward God. More and more people each year are being trained as spiritual directors. Spiritual Directors International, a collegial interfaith membership group for spiritual directors, now has more than six thousand members, most of them in North America but many on other continents too.

I practice spiritual direction, train and supervise directors, and am immersed in spiritual direction at New College Berkeley (where I supervise the group spiritual direction program) and elsewhere. In addition to training spiritual directors, I have taught in programs that train psychotherapists and paraprofessional counselors, and I appreciate the ways in which practitioners in those fields participate in soul cultivation, whether or not they do so from within a faith tradition. The distinctive gift of spiritual direction is its primary commitment to directing people's attention to the presence of the Holy Spirit in their lives.

Many people find the word *direction* problematic. Some of us who have been trained and serve as spiritual directors feel that the word poorly matches the gentle listening practice we engage in. It sounds authoritative, skirting close to the spiritual danger of one person presuming to come between another person and God, conveying God's word to the other or brokering the relationship in some way. Yet the word *director* is what the tradition has used, and it remains.

Given its linguistic stature and longevity, it seemed to me that knowing the origin of the word *direction* in spiritual direction would be helpful, but that origin was elusive.[3] A few years ago when I was asking everyone I thought might know about it, Father Justin Sinaites, the knowledgeable librarian of St. Catherine's Monastery, told me that the first use of the word that became *director* seemed to be in a treatise known as "The Shepherd," a letter to spiritual directors appended to John Climacus's early seventh-century book *Ladder of Divine Ascent*.[4] Climacus wrote, "A ship with a good navigator [or pilot] comes safely to port, God willing."[5]

The word for director is the Greek *kubernetes*, used in the New Testament to refer to a ship's pilot (Acts 27:11; Revelation 18:17), as well as to the spiritual gift of guidance or "administration" (1 Corinthians 12:28). From this ancient word a number of English guidance-related words derive, including *gubernatorial, cybernetics* and, dropping the Greek root, *spiritual director*. The word also exists in academic life as the Kappa of the honorary Phi Beta Kappa Society, a name that weaves together love of wisdom (*philosophia*), style of life (*bios*) and skill in navigation (*kubernetes*) as the crowning glories of a virtue-generating education and, indeed, features of a cultivated life.[6]

Piloting imagery captures some core aspects of the experience of being a spiritual director. A harbor pilot boards a ship to help a captain bring the ship to port, and a spiritual director helps a person steer the ship of his or her life more and more toward God. The focus is on the journey of the captain and the ship, not on the pilot. The pilot contributes knowledge of the terrain, weather, currents and what is helpful in navigating them.

In spiritual direction it is the other's life that is of focal concern, yet the director brings to the relationship knowledge about Christian faith and life as well as specialized training and experience. We accompany directees by God's grace. The pilot does not see the whole of the other's journey or even the whole of the ship, nor does the spiritual director. The pilot might say, "There are strong tidal currents here at this time of day." A spiritual director could say, as mine did, "The waves of grief are strong now but will subside as grace promotes healing."

The pilot and the director do not override the agency or responsibility of the person they are helping. A spiritual director directs the other's attention to the presence and activity of God, who sets the directee's course. Long-term engagement in spiritual direction is profoundly cultivating of a spiritual life.

SPIRITUAL DIRECTION IN THE FIELD: AN ILLUSTRATION

Not everyone takes up regular, formal spiritual direction, yet people in many situations have been helped, even briefly, by another person directing their attention to God. One story of direction in the midst of everyday life is told by Father Gregory Boyle in his book *Tattoos on the Heart*.[7] Father Boyle is a Roman Catholic priest and so is familiar with the church's long tradition of spiritual direction. He works with gang members in downtown Los Angeles, helping them create safer, better lives, in practical and spiritual ways. He also comes to know and love them.

Boyle wrote about listening to "Willy," a young man who lives in the barrio and is a peripheral member of a gang who "wants more to regale you with his exploits than to actually be in the midst of any."[8] One evening as he listened to Willy, Father Gregory enabled Willy to listen.

Father Gregory, called "G" by the boys, was just leaving his office at eight o'clock when Willy sneaked up on him as he started his car. Willy said his stomach was empty, and he asked G for some money to buy food.

Father Gregory responded that his wallet, too, was empty. He addressed Willy as "Dog," explaining to the reader that a dog is "the one upon whom you can rely . . . the person who has your back."[9] He invited Willy into his car and told him he'd try to get him some money from the ATM.

Willy got into the car, and Father Gregory wrote that he was "a life force of braggadocio and posturing—a thoroughly good soul—but his confidence is outsize, that of a lion wanting you to know he just swallowed a man whole." In his midtwenties, Willy is "a quintessential homie con man who's apt to coax money out of your ATM if you let him."[10] Father G. let him.

The priest parked near an ATM at a minimarket and told Willy to stay in the car while he went inside to get some cash. He didn't want Willy to run into anyone from a rival gang, and a minimarket at night is just the place a violent encounter could happen.

When Father G. was about ten feet from the car on his way to the minimarket, he heard Willy call out to him. Willy mimed that he wanted the car keys so he could turn on the radio. The priest mouthed "no" in response. "Then it's my turn to mime," he wrote. "I hold both my hands together and enunciate exaggeratedly, '*Pray*.' Willy rolled his eyes and sighed, but he held his hands together as though praying and looked toward heaven."[11]

Father G. continued on his way, got the cash and returned to the car:

> Something has happened here. Willy is quiet, reflective, and there is a palpable sense of peace in the vehicle. I look at Willy and say, "You prayed, didn't you?"
>
> He doesn't look at me. He's still and quiet. "Yeah, I did."
>
> I start the car.
>
> "Well, what did God say to you?" I ask him.
>
> "Well, first He said, '*Shut up and listen*.'"
>
> "So what d'ya do?"
>
> "Come on, G," he says, "What am I sposed ta do? I shut up and listened."[12]

As Father G. drove Willy toward his home in the barrio, he noticed that Willy seemed humble, not trying to convince Father G. of anything. The conversation continued:

> "So, son, tell me something," I ask. "How do you see God?"
>
> "God?" he says, "That's my dog right there."
>
> "And God?" I ask, "How does God see you?"
>
> Willy doesn't answer at first. So I turn and watch as he rests his head on the recliner, staring at the ceiling of my car. A tear falls down his cheek. Heart full, eyes overflowing. "God . . . thinks . . . I'm . . . *firme*."
>
> To the homies, *firme* means, "could not be one bit better."[13]

Father G. helped Willy stop, attend and open his heart. In the listening, there was an encounter. Father G. trusts that God—the God who is the Way, the Truth and the Life—will speak when Willy listens. As Willy continues to listen to himself, God and Father Gregory, he will be formed more and more by God. Attachment will spring from attention; formation will follow encounter. But first, there is love. As Father G. wrote, "Not only does God think we're *firme*, it is God's joy to have us marinate in that."[14]

MARINATION AS FORMATION

It's God's joy for us to marinate in his loving regard. Spiritual directors help people register their God-given belovedness, and that's what Boyle did for Willy. It is a sacred trust to behold another's holy belovedness. When we do so, we, the beholders, also marinate in grace.

This is something we can all do for others. We can extend contemplative listening, allowing ourselves to be sounding boards for the heart of God and the heart of the other person. It is also a practice that has been formalized over centuries, in which a person seeks the holy listening of another person who feels called, gifted, skilled and committed to offering it.

Spiritual direction is a formal, asymmetrical and caring relationship. The listener and the one listened to are in identifiable roles and engage with one another in distinct and different ways; this makes the relationship asymmetrical. It's a relationship of care: how the listener orients toward the speaker is affected by regard for the speaker. Also, how the speaker speaks is affected by how the listener listens and responds. The roles are distinct but interdependent. A person is listened into speech as another is drawn into listening.

Father G. is a priest, and Willy is a young man in the community of people that Father G. serves. That gives their relationship a formal context. Their relationship is asymmetrical and caring. Father G. helps Willy listen to God, and Willy doesn't assume the role of helping Father G. listen for God. But Willy's experience of God touches Father G.'s heart, just as the story moves us as we read it.

Although spiritual directors are called into particular roles with directees, they are not on a higher spiritual plane. Together we bow down and look up to God. When I've listened to a person's experience of God, I take it to prayer and to my own time of being directed so that I can marinate in it.

Marination is formative. Cooking marinades cause the tissue of meat to break down and absorb more moisture. The process involves acids, enzymes and sometimes oils and spices that are potent, so instructions usually include something about the container, which should be made of materials that don't interfere with the effect of the marinade on the meat, like glass, instead of plastic, which can be altered by acid.

Our incarnation means that we are subject to marination. We are steeped in our culture—bidden or unbidden—and we can be aware that we soak in God's goodness and grace. Spiritual direction is a discipline that explicitly draws our attention to that in which we are bathed and by which, perhaps, we are pickled. The practice creates a container that aids the marination. Jean Bolen, serving as my director, helped me notice the grief with which I was suffused. Her focused attention helped me see more: though steeped in grief, I was also surrounded and buoyed by grace.

Had ours been a symmetrical relationship, I believe I would not have discovered my deeper experience. Jean held the focus on my experience, and mutuality didn't extract me from it through interest in her life, concern that I was taking too much attentional time, or the discomfort of emotional nakedness before a close acquaintance. Asymmetry is a distinctive gift of the discipline. Our relationship was not mutual, but it was caring. I'm sure my experience shaped her response, and her stance of care allowed the light of insight to be cushioned by warmth. I could enter into the depths of grief knowing that I was in loving hands—hers and God's.

The formal contours of the relationship created a caring container that enabled me to marinate in God's grace. There were boundaries related to space, time, roles and practice that allowed for freedom.

Space. We met in a quiet, professional space with minimal visual and auditory distractions. The placement of the chairs encouraged face-to-face encounter across a comfortable distance.

Time. There was a set time for our meeting—neither too short nor too long. The soul does notice time, often staying closed if time is too brief and feeling overexposed when time is open-ended. Dr. Bolen and I met regularly, allowing me to feel prepared for the time together. Those times were recorded on my personal calendar and were distinct from other kinds of time in the weeks of my life.

Roles. My director and I observed our roles. She offered competence, confidentiality and a commitment to use her experience, skills and awareness for the sake of my soul. I came with a trusting willingness to explore the depths of my experience and listen for God, the true director.

Practice. In contrast to the psychotherapeutic professions, spiritual direction is a nonregulated, nonlicensed religious practice. There are ethical guidelines among collegial groups of spiritual directors, but no professional requirements or monitoring of qualifications and ethical practice. However, it is a caring art with expectations for practice that are of the highest order, humanly and spiritually.

Spiritual direction is a gift that can be received outside of the formal discipline, as we see with Father G. and Willy, just as praying with Scripture may happen spontaneously outside of a formal practice. That is grace. We can also set our hearts to seek grace through regular spiritual disciplines. Over the years, I have partaken of spiritual direction as a perennial, rather than seasonal, addition to the life God is cultivating in me.

FOR REFLECTION

1. What spiritual disciplines help you listen to your soul and to God? What people? Consider how a particular person or persons

are crucial to one of your spiritual disciplines (for instance, in worship).

2. In reading about my experience with a spiritual director, did you recognize the interaction as similar to a relationship in your life? Consider the similarities and differences.

3. Is there someone in your life who regularly serves as a "pilot" for your soul as you seek God? If there isn't, and you're interested in finding such a person, read "Guidelines for Finding a Spiritual Director" in the Appendix.

10

Rooted and Grounded by Friendship

Let us be grateful to the people who make us happy;
they are the charming gardeners who make
our souls blossom.

Marcel Proust, *Pleasures and Days*

*L*ove pulses at the heart of the cultivated life, its beat becoming especially pronounced when mortality is faced. Nearing the end of his life in midlife, Peter Ogle wrote, "I have no particular sense of what I want my last days or weeks to look like. I've lived my bucket list—been everywhere I wanted to go and done all I needed to do. I've been blessed in life beyond measure, to which I hope this blog is testament. I now mostly want to be around family and friends."[1]

A week later he added that in recent days he'd "had the privilege and challenge of saying good-by to people I love. I will continue to do so in what time I have. When all pretense and artifice is stripped away, when every encounter brings with it a sense of finality, some real communication begins."[2] Peter enjoyed new depth with loved ones, even at the end.

CULTIVATING FRIENDSHIP

Peter was a writer who used a computer to weave community. My mother had a landline phone and the US Postal Service. Left behind when she died were her well-worn address book and a stack of greeting cards she had collected to send to people. Some of Mom's very last acts from her hospital bed involved reaching out to those she loved, asking about their lives and then telling her own stories woven from her full though circumscribed days.

Peter Ogle and my mother were soul gardeners for their friends and also relished being tended by friends. They attended to people and were attached to them, keeping their relational gardens in good repair. Both of them made us laugh and cry, stretching our hearts, even in their final days.

Studies of health and well-being conclude that social ties are health-generating (salutogenic), while isolation tends to foster illness (pathogenic). Some of us are constitutionally better equipped than others for friendship, but the cultivation of friendship is a spiritual discipline available to everyone.

Australian palliative care nurse Bronnie Ware works with people who have chosen to die in their own homes. She has asked her patients whether they had regrets as they approached death. Letting friendships lapse was one of the top five regrets people mentioned at the ends of their lives.

People regret the loss of friendship, yet our culture offers little instruction about maintaining friendships. Doing so is a spiritual discipline. This chapter presents a view of friendship as a discipline, and the next offers practical suggestions about cultivating it.

Ware writes that many of her patients "had become so caught

up in their own lives that they had let golden friendships slip by over the years. There were many deep regrets about not giving friendships the time and effort that they deserved. Everyone misses their friends when they are dying."[3]

The love attachments that shape us—with God, family, friends and all those who are significant in our lives—are woven into the fiber of our being. Indeed, Ware claims that at the very end of life, love and relationships are the whole of what matters. Young or old, the ecology of our lives is affected by our ties with other people. Some of those relationships are given, and many are chosen; some attachments are healthy, while others are not and stand in need of change.

After I've spoken to groups on the subject of friendship, I'm sometimes told that what really hit home is a quote usually attributed to Tennessee Williams: "Friends are God's way of apologizing to us for our family."[4] Though this sentiment resonates for many people, it's also true that among our family members we may have friends. My mother worked steadily through the years to create a friendship with me, and I have an ornament she gave me that proclaims that truth: "Always my daughter; now, too, my friend." Our blood relationship was given and immutable. Our friendship was a gift, choice and discipline.

Years ago when I was preparing to teach a graduate theological seminar about friendship, the sociologist Robert Bellah, my mentor and friend, told me that "friendship is the most important, least examined area of human life." He was speaking as a social scientist, but friendship also may be the most overlooked important relationship in the field of spirituality. A staple concern of classical philosophy, and core to Greek and Roman thinking about how goodness is shaped in the human soul, friendship has slipped into neglect.

Examining friendship as the final spiritual practice in this book is an act of retrieval. It is an heirloom plant in the gardens of our lives, of ancient provenance, precious and in need of tending.

An Ordinary and Neglected Practice, and a School of Virtue and Love

For centuries philosophers have wrestled with a paradoxical cry of the heart attributed to Aristotle: "O my friends, there is no friend."[5] In keeping with his own theory, the philosopher may have been longing for a soul friendship in the midst of other friendships, something deeper and stronger than a buddy kind of friendship based on pleasure, or a networking one based on utility. Aristotle wrote of this truer friendship as a school of virtue,[6] and in the twelfth century the Cistercian monk Aelred of Rievaulx called it a school of charity.[7] Reflecting on how political conflicts ravage our lives today, Milan Kundera declared that "unlike the puerile loyalty to a conviction, loyalty to a friend is a virtue—perhaps the only virtue, the last remaining one."[8]

Over the years as I've asked people about their experience of friendship, the responses sound like Aristotle's lament: "I had a best friend, but she suddenly broke off the relationship and I don't know why. It's been years, and it still hurts. My suffering is lonely. There's no place to speak about a broken friendship. It makes me question friendship."

Men say, "I wish I had close friends like women seem to have. What I have are buddies, people I see at work or on the tennis court. The relationships are pretty shallow. When I go to a new workplace, the buddies from the old job fall away. How do people have friends?"

A school is a place of formation, of cultivation. That's what such friendships can be. Being in school requires time and effort, resources we allocate more and more to work. In fact, as women have entered the workforce in larger numbers, there's some suggestion that women, too, experience more relationships that are networked or collegial and, like men, have fewer friendships. In a 2013 interview, Jane Conrad and Marilyn Lovell, wives of Apollo 13 astronauts, spoke of their decades-long friendship and how unusual it seems these days. Jane said, "Maybe women today don't need friends like we did." To which Marilyn replied, "They have colleagues now."[9]

It's true that work has superseded friendship in many lives, and social media, so easily accessed in the workplace, give people a taste of broader relationships, but nothing like the relationship the word *friend* brings to mind.

In the mid-twentieth century, Christian literary scholar, friend extraordinaire and armchair theologian C. S. Lewis wrote, "To the Ancients, Friendship seemed the happiest and most fully human of all loves; the crown of life and the school of virtue. The modern world, in comparison, ignores it."[10] Political scientists writing today claim that "the bonds of friendship [have] been eviscerated."[11] Many of my friends and I share these sentiments, seeing friendship as of incalculable worth and beauty yet suffering from neglect—by us and by the culture.

My parents treasured their friends, maintaining frequent contact with them until the ends of their days; their lives were extended as well as enhanced by friendship. Yet when I included my mother's best friend Mary Beaudry in the part of her obituary where the dearly-beloved-left-behind are named, my father said, "It's unusual to mention a friend." Then, on reflection, he added, "But it's how it should be."

WHAT IS FRIENDSHIP AND WHERE IS IT FOUND?

What exactly is friendship? Not easily defined and absent from most encyclopedias, it's a love relationship considered to be ordinary, even unnecessary, experienced privately and usually without examination. This seemingly garden-variety love, less prone than other kinds of love to hellish and heavenly extremes, is broadly defined as a mutual, egalitarian, nonsexual, private, free relationship of uncertain duration and variable intensity.

Friendship is trumped in adult life by the demands of work and family within a culture of fragmented relationships and an ethos of self-determination. These cultural features serve the current socioeconomic structure. Turning down an appealing job offer in order to continue living near a friend is rare and baffling. People say, "We're *just* friends."

Friendship has been called unnecessary. Lewis's response to that was "Friendship is unnecessary, like philosophy, like art, like the universe itself (for God did not need to create). It has no survival value; rather it is one of those things that give value to survival."[12] Even in affluent societies, we too often live to work, rather than work to live.

Friendship can be an entertaining subject for a situation comedy and—in life as on television—is a primary relational focus for children, adults in unusual family-absent situations like the military and the monastery, and those in transition between family commitments, including the final season of life. It is also consistently found to promote thriving among the elderly.

Despite its persistence in human life through the ages, we regard friendship as an accessory and avocation in an adult's vocational life. It is also not seen as central to spirituality, existential concerns or self-realization. Seldom does friendship move to center stage. We have no ceremony marking its inception and none marking its dissolution, nor does our culture offer us any analysis of how to sustain, nurture, correct and shape friendship. When a friendship breaks, we are left with an assortment of feelings, few tools for understanding those feelings and no mechanisms for repair, retrieval or mourning.

Children, on the other hand, are evaluated in terms of their abilities to form friendships. Adolescent pals and buddies are recognized as developmental necessities, and psychologists have linked the capacity to form adolescent friendships with eventual adult abilities to work cooperatively and establish families. Childhood friendship is viewed as a kind of rocket booster launching people into adulthood, then falling away as mature orbit is achieved.

OF NO EARTHLY USE?

We engage in only minimal public reflection about the shape and development of friendships, religious institutions grant friendship scant programmatic or pulpit attention, and secular spiritual movements, on the whole, neglect this relationship. Churches often cultivate spiritual community, a form of neighbor love and a precious but different gift and discipline from friendship. Within the church's teachings, friendship is dwarfed by the loves of God, neighbor and family.

Perhaps our lives, so dominated by the demands of work and family, have little room for a relationship so lacking in measurable usefulness. Studies of students at elite universities have found they are so focused on academic advancement leading to workplace positioning that they are forgoing the cultivation of relationships that might lead to marriage. It's not a great leap to imagine that if they are unwilling to invest precious time in developing potentially long-term romantic relationships, they certainly may calculate friendship to be too costly as well. One woman said, "If I'm sober, I'm working."[13]

Committed relationships are seen as obligations that interfere with getting ahead and investing in one's own development, so briefer, shallower connections are becoming normative. The danger exists that social media, rather than facilitating deeper connections, might simply allow a kind of "friendship hookup," brief and emotionally unencumbered, granting a taste of connection as well as some networking capital.

Friendship is and has always been enticing and confusing, in our experience and in our thoughts. Cicero is said to have claimed that friendship "is a kaleidoscopic and complicated thing."[14] Perhaps that accounts for the persistent, though thin, literature on the subject. Like a kaleidoscope, friendship may be seen as enjoyable and inconsequential, mesmerizing and fluid, yet bereft of allure when subjected to analysis.

A DANGEROUS ATTACHMENT

It might be argued that we can be mature adults and righteous Christians without particular friendships, marriage or children. For example, cloistered monks and sisters have trusted that loving God and neighbor is sufficient for spiritual development. Yet deeming friendship inessential or not useful seems an insufficient explanation for the gross neglect of the subject in cultural, critical and ecclesial thought.

Some traditions have viewed this ordinary love as hazardous: It might jeopardize democratic participation in community, interfere with obedience to authority and compete with the biblically commanded spiritual loves. Friendship is unfairly preferential and has the power to touch and change us and society. When divinely commanded love (*agapē*), in its God-devoted and neighborly forms, is deemed the proper love of the Christian, then the particular, preferentially chosen and exclusive love of a friend (*philia*) may be seen as dangerously selfish and spiritually distracting.

Philosophers and theologians, including the influential thinkers Søren Kierkegaard and Anders Nygren, as well as many Christian communities through the ages, have made the argument that friendship love is incompatible with the ideal of charity.[15] While this view is seldom spoken today, it may have contributed to our society's neglect of friendship and the absence of a robust Christian conversation about friendship as a spiritual discipline.

Particular friendships within cloistered communities, church congregations, political parties, neighborhoods, schools and other communities can lead to dissension, favoritism, injustice and varieties of temptation. Because of such fears, cloistered religious communities have had, and some still have, rules against particular friendship.

In a spiritual direction session, the new senior pastor of a large Protestant church lamented that it wasn't possible to have friends in the congregation: "My family can't even have people in the church over for a meal because it would give the impression of favoritism, and people would be jealous. It's so hard, because opening our home to friends from church has been a big part of our family life."

While bans on particular friendships seem extreme, we can understand the concerns that led to those rules. All of us are familiar with the pain of being excluded from a particular friendship within a community. If we approach two of our friends who have been chatting and see them turn their backs on us, our sense of well-being takes a blow. We feel excluded and unwanted. Jealousy and shame may rear their heads, possibly followed by malevolent thoughts and retributive action (like *I'll just ignore them the next time I see them*).

There are costs associated with friendship love, costs that require spiritual work and discernment. How can we cultivate a healthy variety of loves in the gardens of our lives—love of God, neighbor, self and also of friends and family? How can friendship be a spiritual discipline that allows for the stretching, nourishing and cleansing of our souls?

Even if we embrace the value of friendship, we know that this kind of love cannot be commanded. A civic, educational or ecclesial leader can encourage friendship, but no authority can order two people to be friends. Neighbors, yes; friendly, also yes. But deep friendship with another person is beyond the control of authority. No one else can control the establishing, flourishing or even ending of such a friendship.

Jesus formed friendships that were beyond the control of and also seriously threatening to the authorities of his culture. It was with the help of a small group of friends that he changed the world. He also endorsed friendship in words, calling his followers, and us by extension, "friends" (John 15:15). Though his friends certainly didn't understand all of what he told them, they took authority-defying risks inspired by their love for him.

People claim that a small group of committed people can change the world, and, in fact, that's the only force that can actually do so. This, of course, can happen for good or ill. A spirituality of cultivation can bring friendship into the larger space of prayer and moral reflection where its nurture and correction can take place.

QUANTIFIABLE AND MANAGEABLE NETWORKS

Though our culture lacks a vigorous conversation concerning friendship, we do have a large and growing field of study concerning the social networks that increasingly impinge upon our lives. For instance, within the public sector it's being recognized that we need more indices of human thriving than merely those of economic growth, and so people's social networks are being examined. A model of this is the 2010 Canadian Index of Well-Being (in part inspired by Bhutan's Gross National Happiness Index), which measures a broad set of social support and isolation factors that affect the nation's thriving at least as much as gross domestic product.

It is interesting that in the published Canadian report, friendship is referenced only in relation to leisure and recreation. In keeping with the overall eclipse of friendship in our public and intellectual culture, the report does not treat friendship as a substantive engagement shaping people's lives in the ways that family and work do.[16] So friendship, Aristotle's "school of virtue," is relegated to a category of leisure-time, nonutilitarian activities that also includes hiking and moviegoing.

Friendship is absent from most social science and spiritual formation theory today, while quantifiable, manageable networks receive more and more attention. The world and all of us in it are rapidly being changed by the unfettered expansion of social media along with the simultaneous erosion of neighborhood, community and, perhaps, friendship.[17] We flock to Internet connectivity sites, while we bowl alone. Researchers are concerned that over the past ten years, as social media have flourished, college students have become less and less emotionally connected to others. They cite as evidence of this trend college students' decreasing levels of agreement with the statement, "I sometimes try to understand my friends better by imagining how things look from their perspective."[18]

It is possible that social networking sites are proliferating in part because they can be taken up while one is at work or at home with family. Keeping in touch with "friends" while engaging in other activities can be viewed as a form of time management. We scan our social media while sitting at our work desk or in front of the television with a family member. Getting together face to face with a friend, on the other hand, would be done instead of working and spending time with family. However, when placed on an electronic device, friendship is disembodied and may feel more like entertainment and, as is the case with both civic involvement and religious participation, becomes increasingly optional in our daily life.

In parallel, within Christian circles we consider what it means to "do," "plant" and "grow church," and more and more we pursue these goals by employing networking tools such as social media. In a study of church websites, Lynne Baab, a communication scholar who lectures in pastoral theology, found that congregational websites "often appear circuslike, with an array of information and opportunities, each one trying to be 'sticky' enough to keep the viewer there for a while. The viewer is urged into becoming a consumer of the circus acts."[19]

THE PUBLIC WORLD OF THE WEB

Networks seem appealingly democratic and public, in contrast with the preferential, private aspects of friendship. Many people "friend" quite promiscuously on Facebook, most of us receive friending invitations from acquaintances and strangers, and we have little awareness or concern about who has access to our network activity. Since posts on Facebook are short and public, they are usually of little consequence, reinforcing the view of friendship as inessential and recreational.

The democratic, public aspect of social media brings to mind the monastic preference for democratic and transparent relationships with all in the community, which in the monastery was for the sake of love of God and neighbor. We've certainly seen how social media support democratic access to information during revolutions and situations of public harassment, knowledge of which governments at times try to suppress.

The push toward democratic, public relationships is also apparent today among childhood educators. Some elementary schools and summer camp programs work against the formation of tight friendship pairs. They do so for some of the same reasons particular friendships were banned in monasteries: best friends are exclusive, secretive and potentially subversive.[20] The message continues to be that friendship may be not only inessential but dangerous too.

Networks, by contrast, seem safer, easily accessible and more useful. The largest example today of a social network is Facebook, which in mid-2014 was the world's second largest "country" (closely trailing China) with more than 1.32 billion users,[21] and whose cyber-territory is visited at least once a day by more than 60 percent of its population.[22] Culture is being shaped by Facebook, yet the social virtues it privileges are less clear than the *agapeic* ones (loves of God and neighbor) of monasteries or the inclusively democratic community of summer camp.

The "friending" mechanism gives a false impression of the Facebook world. Though Facebook allows a person to have as many as five thousand "friends" (above that you have to create a fan site), the average user has 142 so-called friends and is in regular contact with only four to seven of them. These numbers are consistent with community studies indicating that people are capable of stable interpersonal relationships in village numbers (around 150), and also with studies that find most people maintain two to six "strong tie" relationships.[23] Of those two to six close relationships with people we are in touch with weekly or thereabouts, it is estimated that half are friends. The other half is composed of spouses, partners, parents, siblings, children, coworkers, fellow members of clubs, neighbors, and professional advisers and consultants.[24]

Networked connectivity increasingly creates an electronically modified relational monoculture within which soul friendship loses social and spiritual "capital." Even so, this hardy heirloom plant continues to enliven the heart's desires and season our days.

Friendship in the Gardens of Our Lives

The Gospel accounts of Jesus' life are told in eighty-nine short chapters, little more than one hundred pages. Few particular relationships in his life get repeated attention, and we read of only a handful of people receiving home visits from him. But his friends in Bethany were given that attention.

Lazarus was the quintessential silent type, Mary enigmatic, and Martha, forthright and strong, was a "sturdy shelter" of a friend (Sirach 6:14)[25] for the man with "nowhere to lay his head" (Matthew 8:20). Jesus' friends tended to his needs and attended to who he was. How right that as he faced death, he stepped out of the circus of being hunted by the authorities and into the garden of friendship's embrace. His friends fed him, washed his feet and anointed him with oil (John 12). It was a friendship—particular, selective and mercifully loving.

Friendship is a form of attachment and requires attention. Un-measured time and freely given attention are aspects of the garden and of friendship. Discipline, too, is needed for attunement and reattunement to the health of relationships and gardens.

In this book you have met people I knew as they were dying, specifically my parents and Peter Ogle. They lived right up until they died and, like Jesus, practiced friendship until the end. Friend-ship's love enabled friends to gather around Jesus, Peter Ogle and my parents in the whole reality of grief and joy. "The house was filled with the fragrance of the perfume" (John 12:3).

FOR REFLECTION

1. Think about your friendships. Who are your buddies and net-working connections or colleagues, and what are those relation-ships like?

2. In addition to these buddies and colleagues, think of one or two long-term friends who are soul friends for you. Describe the nature of the relationship. What is the bond like? How is it maintained? What is the gift of that soul friendship?

3. What interferes with friendship in your life? What aids it?

Practicing Friendship

*I have called you friends, because I have made known
to you everything that I have heard from
my Father. . . . I chose you.*

FRIENDSHIP MATTERS. So say our hearts, though friendship is neglected by the culture, spiritual formation programs, colleges, seminaries, workplaces and religious institutions.

Where are we to turn when we would like wisdom about cultivating friendship in our lives? Among Amazon's offerings on the subject, we find a mix of children's books, books about the friendships of animals and a number of how-to books. Novelist Amy Bloom has declared *George and Martha*, a children's book about hippo friends, "the greatest book about friendship ever written."[1] She may be right.

Less prominent is the tenacious but thin literature about the value of "spiritual" (or "soul") friends[2] who enrich our lives, shape our characters and change communities and the world. Soul friends are *anam cara* in Gaelic, and that is the title of John

O'Donahue's best-selling book from the late 1990s, the last widely read book in this genre.

FRIENDSHIP AS SPIRITUAL DISCIPLINE

Do we who value spiritual thriving live as though we believe that friendship shapes persons and the world, or do our choices indicate that we regard it as a morally neutral, private accessory in a full life? Do our lives, like those of thinkers from the classical and Christian past, show that we cultivate friendship as a priority in our lives and a blessing to the world?

In a garden, each organism affects the health and cultivation of the garden as a whole. Similarly, when we witness a friendship we are changed. The friendship between Ruth and Naomi rippled through the community in Bethlehem and down through David's lineage to Jesus. Our lives have been affected by reading how Jesus shared love with friends.

Today there is confusion about the state of friendship in our culture among the few social observers who write about it. Some writers wonder about the quality of friendships in an age of social media. For example,

> It may be true that deep friendships are declining. Or perhaps it is true, as some have argued, that online community is creating a renaissance of friendship in our time. Or maybe social networking and other forms of online connection are a desperate response to the trends toward isolation in Western countries today. Or perhaps the enthusiastic embrace of all these forms of electronic communication isn't so much a desperate response as a simple indicator of the deep truth that people thrive on connections with others, and they will use whatever means are available to build and sustain relationships.[3]

Some people who study social media are concerned that they foster shallower and briefer relationships that do not cultivate character. Of course, this is not necessarily so. Any communications medium can facilitate the spiritual discipline of friendship, and, conversely, face-to-face relationships can be shallow and bereft of spiritual cultivation.

People of faith are more familiar with the language of spiritual discipline than that of "school of virtue," but both concepts concern the formation of character through practice. All spiritual disciplines depend on and work with our human faculties and the conditions of our lives. This is true of a primarily attentional practice like mindfulness or lectio divina and also of attachment-fostering relational practices like spiritual direction and soul friendship.

When we engage in regular practices that focus and shape our attention toward God, we work in concert with the realities of the human condition. Because we are embodied, posture can help us enter into a spiritual discipline—for instance kneeling, bowing or closing our eyes in prayer. We use our bodies to speak prayers, sing hymns, inhale incense and register God's grace in tears and laughter. Do we meet our friend with our whole self and focused attention?

We exist in time, so practices related to the day and the hour are common, such as weekly worship, morning prayers and mealtime thanksgiving. What time do we give to friendship?

We exist in space, so certain spaces are assigned sacred activities, as with a sanctuary space, a hilltop or a prayer closet. Where does friendship take place in our lives?

We respond to beauty and decorate ourselves and our environment with things that help us engage in spiritual disciplines—prayer shawls and beads, altars, labyrinths, stained-glass windows, holy banners, kneelers at pews. What ornaments our friendship and marks its preciousness?

And we are social creatures, worshiping in communities of presence, memory and imagination, and cultivated by the relationships we choose. How do we nurture friendship in the midst of our other relationships?

All these dimensions of our humanity can be called upon to fortify the discipline of friendship, and the more we engage with our whole selves, the deeper the reach of formation. In choosing a spiritual discipline, we exert force against the ubiquitous and often invisible forces of the culture by which we are also shaped: those that would have us connect with friends only virtually, accord no regular time or place to the relationship, do nothing to mark the specialness of friendship, and simply walk away from friendship when it conflicts with other relationships we hold dear.

Friendship is an essential dimension of our humanness and of God, in whose image we are formed. This commonplace part of our lives, when it is taken up as a spiritual discipline, cultivates attachment and even holiness, countering the circus forces that push us to be observers or performers. In the preface to his *The Spirit of the Disciplines,* Dallas Willard wrote, "My central claim is that we *can* become like Christ by doing one thing—by following him in the overall style of life he chose for himself."[4] Jesus' lifestyle included living among friends.

THE SHAPING OF A FREE AND INTIMATE LOVE

The etymology of the word *friend* sheds light on the practice of friendship. It derives from two Old English words: *freo,* which meant free, not in bondage, and *freon,* which meant love.[5] From these words, then, *friend* means a free lover, or one who loves freely. This is illustrated by the gifts my mother gave me that affirmed that while I had always been and would be her daughter, I became her friend. Being her friend was not a given. It was a freely chosen relationship that we tended.

Friendship today stands in clear distinction from family relations, in our minds and language. The contemporary secular view of marriage is based on romance in private and contract in public, "with the proviso," some scholars claim, "that the contract will dominate one's private life once the heat of romance runs out of fuel."[6] For the church, marriage is a holy and enduring covenant witnessed by God and community. Friendship, however, is a relationship of freely chosen intimacy, not bound by romance, blood, contract or sacrament, and not expected—although it's possible—within marriage and family.

Another English word for friend is *kith*. *Kin* and the seldom heard *kith* are contrasting words, one indicating family and the other, friends. *Kith*, related to the Old English word *couth*, is familiar for the role it plays in the word *uncouth*, which means unknowing, clueless, not adequately socialized into the culture's ways. Therefore one's *kith* (friends) are those who know one and who do indeed have a clue, and it's this level of intimacy that causes betrayal or rejection by a friend to cut so deeply.

The *Oxford English Dictionary* lists an obscure definition of *kith* as "knowledge communicated." Particular friends share with each other who they are and what they know. The sharing is mutual and takes place within a protected sphere of care and commitment. For millennia people have written that to look in a friend's eyes is to see a second self, a mirror to one's soul. In contemporary psychological theory, trusting self-disclosure and communicated empathy are the noted components of intimacy. Such intimate knowledge between friends is rooted in trusting self-revelation and trustworthy love. Friendship "at all levels is built upon generous sharing rather than skeptical evaluation."[7]

Jesus spoke of communicated knowledge as foundational to
friendship when he told the disciples, "I have called you friends,
because I have made known to you everything that I have heard
from my Father.... I chose you" (John 15:15-16). Freedom, trust and
intimate personal knowledge are crucial components in the friendships that shape our spiritual lives. In spiritual friendships, like
those Jesus shared with his friends, we allow our souls to be heard
and our prayers voiced. Spiritual friendship is a resilient "threefold
cord" (Ecclesiastes 4:12) that braids two human lives together with
that of the Holy Spirit.

That threefold cord is especially necessary in a culture with no
industries to maintain this time-honored relationship; no friendship
medicine, because health among friends isn't viewed as an essential
issue; no friendship law, because friends can join and part without
legal sanction; no organized practices of friendship quality control,
conditioning or emergency supply; and no friendship counseling or
church ministry.[8] There are now "friend doctors," psychotherapists
who teach children how to be friends in a group format, but no
comparable help for adults.

The social neglect of friendship does have a benefit—it preserves
friendship's freedom. Unregulated and unprescribed, friendship
has full license and scope to function as a spiritual discipline. How,
then, do we create spiritual practices that allow for the free flow of
love toward God and a soul friend?

To be selected as another soul's "own society" is a gift beyond
our control,[9] so to recognize the holy gift underlying the discipline
is crucial. Also, the gift of spiritual friendship requires cherishing
through discipline.

The suffix -ship means "the making of." Friendship is the making
of a relationship of free love; therein lies its beauty and its fragility.
It is shaped while it unfolds, like the plant in the tended garden.

This is soulcraft, spiritual formation, the cultivated life in which we participate.

THE PRACTICES OF SPIRITUAL FRIENDSHIP: AN ILLUSTRATION

The more we cultivate the discipline of friendship, the greater our flourishing. Madeleine L'Engle wrote, "Years ago a friend said to me, 'After forty it's maintenance, maintenance, maintenance.' . . . As we do what we can to maintain our bodies, so we must do with our friendships."[10] To emphasize friendship's significance, I draw your attention to Jesus. In particular, we return to his friendship with Martha of Bethany to see how it illustrates the practices of friendship.

Receiving. Jesus and Martha received each other. Martha established the possibility of friendship by welcoming Jesus and his friends into her home: "Now as they went on their way, he [Jesus] entered a certain village, where a woman named Martha welcomed him into her home" (Luke 10:38). Welcoming is a practice of friendship that renders us vulnerable and exposed to others' impressions of our lives and homes and also to our own hopes for the encounter. Attending and tending come into play, listening and beholding become possible.

The more our lives are stretched on the rack of circus polarities—busyness and exhaustion—the less we are inclined to extend welcome to another, and Martha-like hospitality becomes increasingly rare in our work-dominated and privatized lives.

Jesus received Martha's welcome, and that's a practice too. Suspicion, resistance and a desire to be in control can interfere with our receiving. Like the sabbath and each weekly experience of it, friendship itself and every particular welcome within a friendship are gifts. Gifts weave connection, interdependency and expectations of reciprocity, which can at times feel burdensome. How much easier it might seem to dodge another's gift of welcome.

There are knickknacks imprinted with the statement "Friends are the people you can call at three in the morning." Martha and Jesus were round-the-clock friends.

Trusting self-disclosure and communicated empathy. The reciprocal practices of intimacy in friendship are trusting self-disclosure and communicated empathy,[11] and we see these in Jesus and Martha's friendship. "She [Martha] had a sister named Mary, who sat at the Lord's feet and listened to what he was saying" (Luke 10:39). Jesus spoke openly in the company of Martha and her siblings. Mary communicated her attentiveness by sitting at his feet and listening while Jesus disclosed things about himself and his mission, confident that the good people listening to him were trustworthy.

Martha, too, trusted Jesus enough to tell him about her growing frustration with serving while her sister sat listening to him. Here we see the rivalry that can arise when one person seems to be preferred over another. "But Martha was distracted by her many tasks ['serving,' *diakonian* in Greek]; so she came to him and asked, 'Lord, do you not care that my sister has left me to do all the work by myself? Tell her then to help me'" (Luke 10:40). Like Jesus, Martha ventured trusting self-disclosure.

Jesus, in turn, met Martha's self-disclosure with a response communicating that he understood her at a deep level: "But the Lord answered her, 'Martha, Martha, you are worried and distracted by many things; there is need of only one thing. Mary has chosen the better part, which will not be taken away from her'" (Luke 10:41-42). Jesus grasped Martha's frustration; even more, he was aware that lurking under the irritation and complaint was her heartfelt desire to be closer to him, as Mary was. Beneath Martha's jealousy was desire for relationship. Jesus welcomed that desire, and their conversation cultivated intimacy.

In friendship, honesty is undergirded by trust. That makes confession and forgiveness possible, ensuring the ongoing psychological health of the relationship and fostering each person's spiritual growth.

Also crucial to friendship is effective communication of empathy. Uncommunicated empathy may feel like indifference or worse to the other person and will stop the flow of honest disclosure. To feel compassion but never find a way to express it does not help one's friend. Jesus let Martha know that he understood what she was feeling.

Cultivating insight: personal and cultural. Jesus didn't merely notice what was going on with Martha; he let her know that he understood she was encumbered by her responsibilities and also by conflicted desires. Martha wished to extend hospitality, which involved serving at the table, but she also longed to sit at Jesus' feet and give him her full attention. Jesus welcomed her in all of who she was, and by the light of Jesus' love, Martha was able to see herself better. A trusted friend helps us grow through self-awareness (akin to mindfulness) and the correction that such insight sets in motion.

Insights flowing from friendship include reflections on cultural expectations. As Jesus encouraged Martha to step out of the woman's role of serving and into the typically male role of listening at the rabbi's feet, he did so as a friend. He addressed their relationship itself and what mattered in it. As he called her twice by name, he extricated her from social conventions that might have interfered with her listening to him. Friendship helps us see ourselves more clearly and also see the cultural rules and assumptions by which we're bound. As a spiritual discipline, friendship transcends, and sometimes ruptures, cultural constraints.

Our hearts are stretched by friendship, and so are our horizons. A friend from another culture or life experience offers us new lenses through which to see ourselves, our lives, our culture and even our God.

Calling us by name. In their first encounter in Bethany, Jesus called Martha by name. He was the rabbi. Their ranks were unequal, and their genders separated them. Nevertheless, Jesus granted Martha his focused attention and the added edification of being addressed by name. Being called by name deepens intimacy and fortifies personal accountability. Anonymous crowds, as can be found in the circus and at village stonings, are dangerous. Responsibility diffuses across the crowd so that people may behave in ways they wouldn't if someone were to call them out by name. When Jesus called Martha by name, affection and moral strength were cultivated.

Martha called Jesus "Lord." Like Peter, Martha later called Jesus "Messiah" when he asked her if she believed that he is the resurrection and the life, the giver of life to all who believe in him (John 11:27). She knew him in a way few others did. Her acknowledgment of who he was mattered to Jesus. Perhaps even for Jesus, intimacy and a kind of strength came from being called by name.

Spiritual friends remind us that God calls us "Beloved." And Jesus calls us "friends." Being called by these names is true confirmation of who we are and are to be.

Accompanying through thick and thin. The friendship between Jesus and Martha began in Bethany when Lazarus was well. At a later time when Lazarus was mortally ill, his sisters sent word for Jesus to come and heal him, but Jesus arrived too late (John 11). However, the friendship between Martha and Jesus was well established before this ordeal, so Martha could candidly express her disappointment with him. Her heartbreak was exacerbated by how well she knew Jesus, and it was from deep grief that she called him "Messiah."

Jesus wept with the sisters outside their brother's tomb. We assume Jesus, "the resurrection and the life," had a larger view of the situation than they did. But friends "rejoice with those who rejoice, weep with those who weep" (Romans 12:15). Jesus joined

Martha and Mary's weeping and then, too, their joy when Lazarus returned to life. Among the other blessings he extended to the sisters, Jesus communicated empathy.

Henri Nouwen writes about such a friend:

> When we honestly ask ourselves which persons in our lives mean the most to us, we often find that it is those who, instead of giving advice, solutions, or cures, have chosen rather to share our pain and touch our wounds with a warm and tender hand. The friend who can be silent with us in a moment of despair or confusion, who can stay with us in an hour of grief and bereavement, who can tolerate not knowing, not curing, not healing and face with us the reality of our powerlessness, that is a friend who cares.[12]

This is spiritual friendship. Jesus, though not powerless, first of all responded compassionately as a flesh-and-blood friend. He was, in fact, an "all-weather friend," and that is what life in a garden requires. Some of us find it easier to be present for our friends when they are experiencing "fair weather," thriving and performing well. Others of us are more comfortable in "foul weather," drawn to friends in their suffering but not in their flourishing.

The honesty of soul friendship helps friends face whatever interferes with being available in all kinds of weather, be it discomfort with misfortune or envy triggered by another's good fortune. Martha was able to confess envy, anger and profound misfortune. The few lines of dialogue we have from Martha and Jesus' conversations show them communicating through all kinds of weather.

Celebration. The sisters and brother in Bethany were the friends Jesus sought out in the days before his arrest and death (John 12:1-8). He knew they would be with him through thick and thin, sunshine and storms. As we know, this was not the case with some of Jesus' other friends. But despite the danger he brought into their home, Martha and her family welcomed him with a last supper, the last supper at which he was the guest who was served. Together they praised God and celebrated Jesus' life, even in the valley of the shadow of death.

They embraced Jesus in love and grief. Mary anointed his feet with costly perfume, perceived by at least one person as a waste of precious resources. Not surprisingly, she was the member of the family who went off script and entered a realm of reverent improvisation, holy time.

As Jesus' feet were washed with nard, Scripture tells us that "the house was filled with the fragrance of the perfume" (John 12:3). Mary's act touched the bodies of all the people in the room as they breathed in the aroma and received the celebration. The garden engages all our senses, and this was garden time—a *kairos* moment.

THE HEART OF FRIENDSHIP

Bronnie Ware, the palliative care nurse who wrote about the top five regrets of the dying, identified having lost touch with friends as one of the most poignant regrets.[13] Friendship as a spiritual discipline also addresses the other four most poignantly held regrets mentioned by Ware's patients.

They regretted having not been true to themselves, often because they succumbed to other people's expectations, and they regretted not having had the courage to express their feelings. A friendship like Martha and Jesus shared, a true friendship of the soul, encourages the expression of our heart as we discover our true self in the mirror of a friend's eyes.

Ware's patients also expressed regret about working too hard. Here the operative word is *too*. Martha's work of serving was a gift that facilitated hospitality and relationship. It became a problem only when it interfered with her heart's desire and became a hollow duty, not a spiritual discipline. A soul friendship requires time, even if that means taking time away from good work.

The other regret Ware cited was not letting oneself be happy. Jesus had a few friends. We each may have a friend—or two, or three—who enables us to know our heart and become the self God is shaping us to be. In this we experience the fruits of the Spirit, and there is joy.

FOR REFLECTION

1. Remember a friendship that is part of your life today. What about the friendship makes it distinctive? Perhaps it is an easy gift in your life; perhaps it perplexes you. Write a paragraph about the friendship, describing your friend and who you are in the friendship.

2. Pray with this friendship. Feel free to use your reflections about the friend you just remembered and described as the "text" for a lectio prayer about the friendship, moving through the steps of lectio divina. As you come to the end of the prayer, consider how you celebrate this friendship.

3. Take up steps one and two for a number of key friendships in your life, allowing yourself to savor them in prayer. With some of them you will be moved to thanksgiving and praise. With some you will be moved to confession. And with some, by God's grace, you may be moved to forgiveness.

BEARING FRUIT AND ENRICHING THE SOIL

The trees of the field shall yield their fruit,
and the earth shall yield its increase.
They shall be secure on their soil;
and they shall know that I am the Lord.

EZEKIEL 34:27

*I*N THE SPIRITUAL LIFE MUCH IS INVISIBLE—the Holy Spirit, the soul and the relationship between them. What we can witness are the effects of grace in human lives and, through those lives, in the world. In cultivation terms, we look for the fruit of spiritual experience while knowing that the Spirit is also at work in ways beyond our ken, in the soil of our lives.

The word *fruit* comes from the Latin word *frui*, which means "to enjoy," so a spirituality of cultivation is about receiving joy. In the twelfth century *fruit* referred to any vegetable or fruit consumed by people and animals, and later it came to be used more narrowly for the fleshy edibles that contain seeds. The fruit is the part of the tree we enjoy. Similarly, the word *fruition* indicated an "act of enjoyment." The notes in our hearts that cultivation imagery sounds are quite different from those struck by our culture's language of production and performance.

CHOOSING FRUITION

Bracingly, the intertestamental Hebrew book of Sirach asserts that all "living things become old like a garment, for the decree from of old is, 'You must die!'" (14:17 NRSV Catholic ed.). The writer then describes the generations of humanity as like abundant leaves on "a spreading tree that sheds some and puts forth others" (v. 18). Each life has its season.

While all people die, not all truly live. For "before each person are life and death, and whichever one chooses will be given" (Sirach 15:17). God will come to meet the person who seeks life, offering the bread of learning and the water of wisdom. This nourishment will cultivate fruit, and the particular fruit "discloses the cultivation of a tree" (Sirach 27:6). We may choose fruition, or we may refuse it.

Jesus spoke about the need to choose life and said about those who know God, "You will know them by their fruits" (Matthew 7:16). The fruit of the spiritual life is joy as well as blessing. It's received and transmitted. We know those who are alive in faith by their fruits, which may not appear in their portfolios or on résumés. We see it in their lives.

Throughout the ages Christian theologians have identified joy as the fruit of faith. Three hundred years ago the Roman Catholic spiritual writer Madame Jeanne Guyon, often imprisoned for her spiritual teachings about the primacy of grace over works, wrote, "The end of our creation, indeed, is to enjoy God, even in this life; but, alas! how few there are who are concerned for this."[1]

Within the Protestant tradition, enjoyment has been privileged in doctrine. The Westminster Shorter Catechism, written in England between 1646 and 1647 and a foundational document of faith in Reformed traditions, poses an opening question about the chief end of our lives. The answer is that we're "to glorify God, and to enjoy him forever."[2] We are to marinate in God's grace, attending to God's glory and receiving joy. The focus is not on what we produce or conjure up. As walking trees we *bear* fruit; we don't manufacture it. We participate with God in transformational enjoyment.

VISIBLE FRUIT

People notice fruit. It draws our attention to the cultivation of the tree. So it is with the trees that we are: we see the fruit they bear. Several times in 2013 a story from Africa was reported by the Associated Press and picked up by newspapers around the world. It's the kind of "human interest" story my mother would have been drawn to and clipped from the newspaper for me. In it I see a walking, fruit-bearing tree.

The story is this: In May 2013 Harrison Odjegba Okene, a twenty-nine-year-old Nigerian cook, was working aboard a tugboat as it towed a Chevron tanker through Nigeria's oil-rich Delta waters. On the morning of May 26, the boat keeled over and submerged to a depth of about one hundred feet. Okene happened to find a room with an air pocket, and as the temperature plummeted he stayed there, listening to fish "eating and fighting" outside the hull. The accident's sole survivor, he spent seventy-two hours underwater before he was rescued.

The story reverberated through the news media, most grippingly in video footage from the rescue diver's camera. Working alongside other divers as they collected the bodies of the other eleven sailors, one diver suddenly felt a hand tap his neck. The viewer shares the perspective of the startled diver as he surfaces through dark water and then focuses on an exhausted man sitting in chest-high water. The diver identifies himself as Bobby, and the dazed survivor says his name is Harrison.

For the three days until his rescue, Okene was sustained by one bottle of Coke and his faith in God. Okene said to a newspaper reporter that as the waters rose during the long hours of his entombment, he began "calling on the name of God. . . . I started reminiscing on the verses I read before I slept. I read the Bible from Psalm 54 to 92. My wife had sent me the verses to read that night when she called me before I went to bed."[3] In particular, he told reporters he was sustained by the verses of Psalm 54:3-6: "O God, by your name save me. . . . The Lord sustains my life" (NAB).

After Okene returned to his home and community at the Redeemed Christian Church of God, his pastor asked him whether "he had used black magic to survive."[4] He was stunned by the question. He had simply prayed to God, using God's Word as his guide. Like Jonah of the Hebrew Scriptures who also survived three days under water, this sailor's troubles did not end with his rescue.

Okene shows us what faith allows: trust that "the Lord sustains my life," even as that life seems to be coming to its end. We are given no guarantee that any words, practice or achievement will ensure health, wealth or longevity. Life does not depend on or benefit from magical attempts to control a deity. But life suffused by faith, hope and love is truly life, even as death closes in. We do not know much about Harrison Okene. Perhaps his love and faith have been steady and strong throughout his life. Perhaps they were forged by the crisis.

Somehow, by grace, in a cold, gradually depleting pocket of air in an upside-down boat on a submerged seabed, Okene remembered his wife and his Lord. He bore the fruit of faith, and we, witnesses to his story, receive joy.

Participating in Holiness

Throughout the psalms that Okene's wife sent to him, the psalmist asks for rescue. Coupled with those pleas are praises. Psalm 57 begs for God's mercy and repeats the phrases "Be exalted, O God, above the heavens. Let your glory be over all the earth" (vv. 5, 11). Okene, like the psalmist, was rescued. We trust he also experienced exaltation even as he extended it to his Lord.

Chapter six addressed what we are able to do to honor the sabbath. Drawing on Isaiah 58, it described the movements of the spiritual discipline of sabbath keeping:

> If you refrain from trampling the sabbath,
>> from pursuing your own interests on my holy day;
> if you call the sabbath a delight
>> and the holy day of the LORD honorable;
> if you honor it, not going your own ways,
>> serving your own interests, or pursuing your own affairs;
>> ... (v. 13)

We stop, turn from our own ways, and turn toward God. These are the movements of the spiritual discipline as we welcome the sabbath and call the holy day a delight.

The next verse, continuing the sentence, begins with a subordinating conjunction denoting an effect of the preceding cause:

> then you shall take delight in the LORD,
>> and I will make you ride upon the heights of the earth;
> I will feed you with the heritage of your ancestor Jacob,
>> for the mouth of the LORD has spoken. (v. 14)

Once we have done our part in sabbath keeping, we simply receive God's grace with joy. For it is God who exalts, provides the feast and gives delight. These two verses of Isaiah 58 are separated by a mere semicolon, marking the shift from "if you" constructions to God's "I will." This is the mysterious mingling of discipline and gift in which we participate.

In the garden, plants extend their roots and branches toward the life-giving elements. But they don't control the rain or the shine. Those animating elements are given. Plants also participate in, yet don't control, their fruit bearing. Fruit is given to those who orient themselves toward life.

EXALTATION

The Isaiah text uses the word *exalt* to capture what we receive when our souls are well watered. The word literally means "lifted high." Exaltation may be part of circus living, for one can be lifted high in rank, pride and power—in one's own eyes and the eyes of others—but this is not the exaltation of which Isaiah speaks. He describes the caring act of God lifting high the one who keeps the sabbath, thereby exalting that person's soul and filling it with joy.

David, who sought the Lord with all his heart, is called "the man whom God exalted" (2 Samuel 23:1). Being lifted on high is the mark of God's blessing to the faithful. God's act of lifting someone up is most poignantly expressed in Isaiah's song of the suffering servant: "See, my servant shall prosper; he shall be exalted and lifted up, and shall be very high" (Isaiah 52:13), though he be "despised and rejected" (53:3). Paul echoes this in Philippians 2:9 when writing about Jesus who was crucified: "Therefore God also highly exalted him." There is no contradiction between exaltation and suffering.

The sabbath puts us in touch with our finitude and smallness as we encounter our limits. Humility and elevation go hand in hand. The word *humus*, soil, is related to the words *humble* and *human*. The prophet Jeremiah assures us that a human being deeply rooted in the soil of God's grace will not "cease to bear fruit" (Jeremiah 17:8), though heat may come and create a year of drought. My dying mother had moments of exaltation as she contemplated her adventurous future, and Peter Ogle, in his final weeks, anticipated "golden days" ahead.

In Scripture, *exaltation* is a relational word. We exalt God, and God exalts the faithful. But we can also exalt ourselves and other gods and be susceptible to the exaltation of others. Idolatry is lifting up and worshiping what ought not to be worshiped. Sometimes it may be a religious leader or group that takes center stage in our hearts. At other times it's something offered to us by the culture, such as fame, identity or acceptance. Most often it is an idolatry of self, which can manifest in multiple forms of self-promotion and self-protection. Jesus summed it up by saying, "All who exalt themselves will be humbled, and all who humble themselves will be exalted" (Matthew 23:12).

Spiritual exaltation is a gift. Harrison Okene may have experienced it. He did not exercise powers of magic or have the power to rescue himself. He bowed down and looked up to God.

Exaltation is, I would argue, the theological word for what psychologists now call "elevation." Social psychologist Jonathan Haidt says that elevation "is elicited by acts of virtue or moral beauty; it causes warm, open feelings ('dilation?') in the chest; and it motivates people to behave more virtuously themselves."[5] For example, when we see a young man offer his subway seat to a pregnant woman, then we are more inclined to act generously. Elevation is a means through which goodness engenders goodness.

In identifying elevation, contemporary social science is exploring an aspect of human experience that biblical wisdom has commented on for millennia, and it always catches our attention. The victimized people who were listened to at South Africa's Truth and Reconciliation Commission hearings experienced moral beauty in the process, and that offered them some healing and even joy. Being listened to changed them. Those who listened experienced moral beauty as they witnessed radically abused people extending radical forgiveness to their abusers. They, too, were uplifted and went on to tell the story.

FEASTING

The movement of the heart toward grace is a hallmark of great literature and is illustrated exquisitely by William Shakespeare's Sonnet 29:

> When, in disgrace with Fortune and men's eyes,
> I all alone beweep my outcast state,
> And trouble deaf heaven with my bootless cries,
> And look upon myself and curse my fate,
> Wishing me like to one more rich in hope,
> Featured like him, like him with friends possess'd,
> Desiring this man's art and that man's scope,
> With what I most enjoy contented least;
> Yet in these thoughts myself almost despising
> Haply I think on thee—and then my state,
> Like to the lark at break of day arising
> From sullen earth, sings hymns at heaven's gate;
> For thy sweet love remembered such wealth brings
> That then I scorn to change my state with kings.[6]

"Thee" may be a person Shakespeare loves, but I like to think of this "thee" as the Holy One. The poet thinks on "thee" when he is discontented with his usual pleasures, desires what others have and views life as a competition he is losing. If life is a circus, he's fallen from the high wire and is shaking his fist at those above.

Then there is the pivot, a turn of attention so often signaled by a conjunction in Scripture and literature—"then," "but," "even so" or in this case, "yet." The speaker's state rises like the lark, an early riser, often the first bird to see dawn breaking over the curve of the earth. To larks is accorded the medieval collective noun *exaltation* (so much more elegant than the goose's *gaggle* and the crow's *murder*).

The reader feels the shift from dark to light, fury to stillness. Love is remembered, and the poet sings hymns at heaven's gate. No longer outcast, he's beloved. Envy dissolves in that sweet light. One imagines that those who know him will experience the difference, as the watered garden he is becomes a spring whose waters will never fail (in keeping with the promises of Isaiah 58:11 and John 4:14).

Research subjects who wrote about experiences of elevation described warm, pleasant or "tingling" feelings (often in their chests) and were more likely to report wanting to help others, to become better people themselves and to affiliate with others.[7] This is *moral emotion*. It's as though the heart is stretched with love, and we see this expansion in the sonnet. The poet's state rises like the lark at break of day, and he sings; he inhales love, no longer nursing envy, and exhales into the world some of the sweetness he has received.

This is the fruit of the cultivated life, wherein the structure of grace is flow: We receive God's grace when we open ourselves to it. Our souls receive a feast and a cleansing. And then that grace flows through us to the world. As God said through the prophet Joel (2:13), "Rend your hearts and not your clothing." Our hearts are stretched by spiritual disciplines, including contemplative listening, sabbath keeping, lectio divina, spiritual direction and soul friendship. Again and again, we become capable of true worship and love.

Sabbath keeping and all other ways of turning toward God hold space for repentance, remembrance and renewal. We bring our humble and beloved selves into the days that God makes holy. From those personal experiences, "repairing the world"[8] may be possible. As the light breaks forth like dawn, the watered garden bears fruit, and the fallow field is rejuvenated. So, too, the grace we have received begins to flow into the world. This is garden living, and spiritual practices are God-given roads into the garden.

MOBILE TENTS AND WALKING TREES

In contrast to the watered garden, the circus of our culture is transient and tented. As the world has become more homogeneous through globalization, we have become increasingly mobile, moving from place to place to find work.

Even in highly community-based societies, young adults move to where the jobs are. A father in Delhi, India, spoke to me with pride about his twenty-something daughter. She recently had gotten an excellent high-tech job in Mumbai. The father's pride was tinged by sadness, for Mumbai is nearly nine hundred miles away from the family home. The daughter had been raised in the home where he and his wife care for his parents and will continue to care for them for the rest of their lives. He values intergenerational living and responsibility, yet he also values his daughter's skills and desire to get ahead in the world. He's torn by conflicting values: the mobility required to climb the career ladder, and the stability of being rooted in family and community.

Circus cultures are mobile, and they're also tented. We often experience ourselves as separate from others even when they are nearby. The faces of our smartphones take us into individual worlds even in our homes, as each family member receives calls and messages on a personal device, and the family as a whole is no longer aware of who is calling or why. Public spaces have become privatized as we move through them, each of us engaged in our own conversations with invisible companions.

Mobile tents are not compatible with the imagery of cultivation, for roots and fruit require stability and connection. Yet it is an article of our faith that the circus exists within the garden, for "neither death, nor life, nor angels, nor rulers, nor things present, nor things to come, nor powers, nor height, nor depth, nor anything else in all creation, will be able to separate us from the love of God in Christ Jesus our Lord" (Romans 8:38-39). Neither circuses nor mobility—geographic, downward or upward—can sever our relationship with Life.

THE LIFE OF SIGNIFICANT SOIL

Cultivation imagery emphasizes rootedness and fruit bearing. Fruit is visible and edible; it brings joy. As the flow of grace cultivates fruit, the walking trees that we are experience God's exaltation and come to the feast. The upward thrust into visible fruit is a joyful manifestation of the gift we receive. We see this in the lives of people who are sustained by God's grace as they work to help the people of the world; skillfully and lovingly care for others; creatively and diligently apply their resources and energies for the world's benefit; and pray when in the desert or the belly of a whale. But fruit bearing is not the only way in which the flow of grace manifests through human life.

T. S. Eliot's "The Dry Salvages," the second of the *Four Quartets,* ends with the hope that after all our striving in this life—including prayer, observance, discipline, thought and action—we might find contentment in the "life of significant soil."[9] The garden image of soil allows a different sightline on cultivation than does fruit, enabling us to contemplate ways that grace flows through a life to become part of what invisibly sustains new life.

Just what is the life of significant soil? The question crosses my mind while listening to people talk about legacy, the gifts they will hand on to others who will come along after their own lives have reached completion. At the meeting of an organization's board of trustees, I listen as people talk about foundations they are creating to carry forward projects they care about that they hope will make the world a better place. With a group of women whose children have left home, I listen as they wonder about their legacies. They trust that what they have transmitted to their children will be a legacy enriching the soil in which future generations grow. Some friends have taken on big final projects or jobs in late midlife, and others have uprooted themselves from comfortable lives so they can serve on the frontlines of human need.

A *legate* is a person with the mission of carrying something between entities—for instance, an ambassador from one country to the other or a delegate from one organization to another. The legate undertakes a journey in order to transport a gift and then usually departs. As our lives mature, we wonder what gifts will be conveyed through us to those who follow. Christians are commissioned with the legacy of Jesus Christ and—as branches in the Vine—hope to be conduits of his grace into the world.

Some legacies take the form of visible fruit. Significant soil, however, is a subterranean spiritual legacy. I would imagine few of us consciously think, *I want to live a life of significant soil.* But many of us hope to be generative, to live a life that will benefit those who will be planted in the soil we leave behind.

Significant soil is humble, for the nutrients in the soil are buried and their origin obscured. Most of us know our parents and perhaps our grandparents, but we don't know the earlier generations of our family whose imprint has been passed down through the centuries. We know our teachers, but we don't know the people who taught them how to teach and care. Though we don't know the previous inhabitants of the soil in which we are planted, we're affected by them, as are the "cathedrals" of redwoods that grow in a circle around the nutrient-rich decaying stump of an original tree.

Poets, spiritual writers, psychologists and philosophers attest to the human longing to make a difference. We may bear fruit in the world that is recognized and shared, and we may even witness the enjoyment it brings. Some of our fruit is immediately received by others, while some falls, decomposes and reenters the soil at our feet, the soil we leave behind. Eliot's image affirms that even the soil remaining where we were once planted, though unseen, matters, and seeds may find life in it.

PARTICIPATING IN SOIL ENRICHMENT

We have considered together some of the spiritual disciplines that counter the attention-fragmenting, attachment-fracturing forces of our culture. They are practices accessible to anyone in any place and time, yet they are often countercultural. They suit walking trees—people rooted and flourishing while on the path with the One who is the Way. They are disciplines that enable us to bear fruit and enrich the soil that outlives us.

The first spiritual discipline we considered was listening, which is essential to all the practices. It enables us to orient and open ourselves to God, to others and to our own hearts. As we listen, we take in what we hear and are changed by it. The one to whom we listen is also affected by our listening attention.

Listening is crucial to all the disciplines in this book. When we pray with Scripture, we listen; in spiritual direction and friendship, we listen. Sabbath is the stop that enables the attention that listening demands. In these movements, attention is engaged and attachments become healthier.

Most of the people you have encountered in this book sought God's grace through various spiritual disciplines. Most of them are not well-known and do not promote themselves as exemplars of spiritual cultivation. Their inventions didn't change the world, nor did their names become brands. My parents, Peter Ogle, people who see me for spiritual direction, the Chinese buffet house workers, the women of the Kassena-Nankena district of northern Ghana, Ben Weir, the men and women who testified before South Africa's Truth and Reconciliation Commission, my students who prayed with Scripture, Father Boyle's young friend Willy, and Harrison Okene are not famous, and the world has not exalted them.

Yet they bore fruit in the world and lived lives of significant soil. As I regard these people, I experience the stretching of my heart that I associate with exaltation. They have changed me, contributing to the soil in which I am planted. Now, I trust, their lives have enriched the soil of your life too.

FOR REFLECTION

1. Consider joy. When have you experienced it, especially in circumstances that were not easy or pleasurable? What do you see of the Holy Spirit's fruit in that experience?

2. Remember a time of exaltation and tell the story, orally or in writing. Was your heart stretched? Do you remember what fruit the experience cultivated?

3. Think about the soil in which you are planted. Which persons do you imagine contributed to its significance? In what ways do you hope to contribute significance to the soil in which those who follow you will live?

Conclusion

LIVING TOWARD COMPLETION

*We know only a portion of the truth, and what we say
about God is always incomplete. But when
the Complete arrives, our incompletes
will be canceled.*

1 CORINTHIANS 13:9-10, *THE MESSAGE*

*B*ABIES ARE SUCH A NICE WAY to start people," declared the
poster in my borrowed office. Above the words was the
beaming face of a baby to prove it. I was at Regent College in
Vancouver, Canada, teaching Christian spirituality to men and
women from around the world and a variety of vocations, ranging
in age from midtwenties to early eighties.

As I worked under the poster each day, I would think, *Yes. And
what's the nice way to complete people?* Students visited me in the
office for academic or personal advising, and others for spiritual
direction. While I listened to them, the poster baby's face and that
of the visitor would both be in my line of vision. By studying with
me, these good people were taking time to consider how Christian

faith shapes a human life in the years between birth and death. That's what this book has considered too.

THE COMPLETE ARRIVES

Two days before turning eighty, the renowned neurologist Oliver Sachs published a newspaper editorial titled "The Joy of Old Age. (No Kidding.)"[1] He wrote that he was beginning to feel "not a shrinking but an enlargement of mental life and perspective" in which he had become more aware of the transient and also the beautiful in life. He was experiencing a multitude of freedoms, including freedom from urgency and freedom to explore what matters to him. He has experienced more and more enjoyment while nearing the completion of his life.

Old age isn't always joyful; nor is young age. The Hebrew and Christian Scriptures tell us that joy is the fruit of the spiritual life, at any age. King David says to God, "You show me the path of life. In your presence there is fullness of joy" (Psalm 16:11). In some of his final words to his friends, Jesus reminds them that he has told them about God's love "so that my joy may be in you, and that your joy may be complete" (John 15:11). Completion may be marked by joy—so say the faithful and the scientific.

In this book about a spirituality of cultivation, there has been an underlying theme regarding completion. Sachs wondered about completion too: "I feel I should be trying to complete my life, whatever 'completing a life' means." Sach's essay shows that his hope of life's completion has to do with continuing to love and to work, commitments that psychology has identified as foundational for a satisfying life.[2] Yet desirable and worthy as love and work are in our lives, faith traditions tell us that the joy of the spiritual life is not the simple sum of those satisfactions. Indeed, the joy of a cultivated life may be experienced even when work fails and love suffers.

The Complete, mentioned by Paul in 1 Corinthians 13, arrives in our lives. It's not an achievement or a destination at which we arrive. In translating 1 Corinthians 13, Eugene Peterson capitalizes "Complete," much as Eliot capitalizes "Life" and as Christian Scripture sometimes renders "Way." Quite a number of people grant uppercase status to "Mystery" too, the grand leading letter in each instance signaling importance and also the possibility of a proper name. Augustine prayed to God with the words "O, Beauty."[3] Given that the One to whom we pray is "the Alpha and the Omega" (Revelation 1:8), Creator of all, perhaps a multitude of word-images for God ought to be crowned with capital letters. All of them are mysteries beyond our control.

Paul writes that what we say and know about God—the Complete—is always incomplete, as are we ourselves. Thomas Merton says too that we are each "a living incompleteness."[4] All of us—individually and corporately, personally and culturally, young and old—are incomplete. Hamlet tells Horatio that human philosophy is incomplete,[5] and that is true of theology as well. We see and see again, as we grasp, lose hold and then resume our seeking. We are incompletenesses embraced by the Complete.

We think of something that's completed as being finished. The word *complete,* from fourteenth-century Middle English, means to fill up or be full, in some languages carrying the connotation of pregnancy's fullness. Intimations of the cultivated life shimmer in these words—a sense of finish and fullness, with a hint of potential.[6]

Joy in Completion

In the lives of people I've watched approach the end with joy, there's a completion of the cup-running-over variety. Sachs knew that joining the words *old age* and *joy* would be jarring for some, so he included "No kidding" in his article's title. In our culture that so values performance, we have a hard time imagining joy in a season of diminished abilities to launch, race and score. At the end of life it becomes difficult to be even a spectator, and for that we have a proliferation of technologies for enhanced vision and hearing but little understanding of what fullness is like in this season.

At memorial services we often hear the Twenty-Third Psalm. The one who walks in the valley of the shadow of death will be led by the Shepherd, fed, anointed with oil, and the cup will run over as mercy and goodness abound. These are images of extravagant love, like that of Mary of Bethany lavishly anointing Jesus' feet with perfume as he approached his death. The prophet Isaiah offers another image of the abundant life: "For you shall go out in joy, and be led back in peace; the mountains and hills before you shall burst into song, and all the trees of the field shall clap their hands" (Isaiah 55:12). The exuberant joy of being led out by God—no kidding.

Being "living incompletenesses" means we're always yearning and devising conscious and unconscious ways to deal with our desire for completion. Participating with God isn't always our first inclination, and we may try to suppress the discomfort of our incompleteness through circus living. The circus can numb the pain of our longing, for performers are wholly focused on the performance. Spectators, too, can be captivated by others' performances, and the efforts of the circus are bent on making that so. For a time, performing and spectating deploy a mute button against our yearning. The calamity, as this book contends, is when the circus becomes dominant in our lives, obscuring the rhythms and nourishment of garden living.

Some of the circus experience of our lives is the stuff of what Oliver Sachs is glad to have outgrown, what he calls the "factitious urgencies of earlier days." These are the manufactured, produced, even artificially contrived rush and press of our culture and the motivating stories we tell ourselves, such as that we need to keep dancing on the high wire, reaching for the next gold ring and keeping up appearances. In the circus culture we parade within the confines of the tent, vault from platform to trapeze or sit in the numbered seats of the bleachers. Part of the illusion is the assumption that our location is identifiable and predictable.

As walking trees, by contrast, we are always in relationship with the Complete who is mystery, always on a path that isn't fully revealed, always sending our roots into what's hidden from view. We participate in our cultivation, which is never finished, never achieved. Throughout the whole of our lives—in old age and all other stages— we lean toward advent, that which is coming toward us.

A grace of my work is that I am with people as they descend from the high wire and shed concern about appearances, when they step out of "factitious urgencies" and settle into their deeper selves, held by God's grace as it's signaled by the candle's light and my attention. The rhythm of spiritual direction allows for a long, reflective look at a life, and people often speak in the imagery of cultivation.

SPIRITUAL DIRECTION IN MIDLIFE: AN ILLUSTRATION

A few months after the deaths of my parents, Sam sat down across from me in the leather chair. He expanded into its wide embrace, seeming to relish the shelter of the hour we would share. During our hours of spiritual direction, I was always struck by the intelligence that played across his face, sometimes communicated in a swift, smiling acknowledgment of irony and at other times in an association from our words to a memory of something experienced or read.

Sam is a man in early middle age and of long-held faith. That faith is evident through its constancy in the midst of fluctuations in his experience. Firmly situated within the Christian flock, Sam follows Jesus, drinks from Scripture and loves the church. He is keenly attuned to the varieties of his religious experience, sometimes adamantine and unquestioning, at other times shaky and elusive.

Our spiritual direction work began in a season of destabilization for Sam. While deeply committed to the church, he had lost his taste for it and was experiencing a restless longing for change. His church community strongly values stability, the spiritual discipline of committing to a particular community and remaining with it through all kinds of seasons and weather. Sam had weathered some rough seasons with the church and had grown unsure that God was calling him to stay there.

Discernment is a core practice of spiritual life. It is also a core practice of life in the garden, for a gardener considers what plants need to be uprooted and moved for the health of the whole garden or for their own well-being, as well as what combination of plants is best according to a variety of criteria. Directees sometimes use garden terms as they speak to me about discernment. One told me she's realized that she's a "shade plant." She flourishes in quieter environments, away from the blaze of light and heat. The realization frees her to be different from many "bright sun" plants of her acquaintance.

Another person refuses to have the Forest Service remove some trees from a mountain property: "Those trees still have life in them. They're not a hazard. I relate to them as I age. Some of my limbs don't function as they did before, but I'm still me and have a lot of life left."

Sam, too, experienced his life in organic imagery. During the year of our work together, he discerned a way forward in his life that held great appeal. It would continue his commitment to Christian community while returning him to a more active stance of faith-based service to the broader society. It would require his uprooting, which would have consequences for other people as well as for him. He prayed over the decision for months, engaging in various forms of prayer to amplify the acoustics of his listening. He felt God's benediction on his hopes, or at least he didn't register God's discouraging him from continuing along the path he envisioned.

Moving forward with hope and zest, Sam encountered a large "Stop" sign planted squarely on the path, blocking him from following his desire. He was surprised and disappointed. The act of stopping hurt, and he doubted his discernment. Had he really heard from God at all? Had he not prayed sufficiently or correctly? Even less speakable and thinkable: Had God led him on and let him down?

Some of Sam's prayer practices withered and ceased. Scripture felt piercing in his state of shattered hope. Ever ethical, Sam didn't allow his letdown to alter his behavior with others. He stayed upbeat and generous, maintaining social involvements and keeping the sadness to himself. In my office he was able to speak about his grief, though even there he wondered if doing so was self-indulgent.

God seemed distant, and Sam was aware that he had taken steps away from God. He felt bruised and had become wary despite his intellectual affirmations of God's goodness and providence. He was no longer casting his nets of hope on the side of the boat where he had expected to find fish. Like the disciples after Jesus' death who went fishing only to experience a long night of fruitless exertion, Sam was discouraged. He gave his nets a rest.

After listening to Sam's discouragement, I asked about any glimmers of grace. That evoked what appeared to be a glint of humor. Meeting my eyes, he said, "I went backpacking."

I expressed interest, and Sam said, "Yeah, I went backpacking. I wanted to get away. The silence was soothing. I wasn't really talking to God—still not sure about all of that. But I felt God was there with me as I walked.

"I came to a section of the forest that had been burned. It was beautiful. There's something about the charred branches scratching the sky that moves me. So angular. Dramatic. It didn't make me sad or give me a feeling of desolation. I was aware of the beauty of the lines and the shades of gray." Sam wistfully described the scene, his eyes no longer meeting mine as they gazed on the remembered forest.

He spoke softly. "I paused and moved closer to a clump of the burned trees, and at their base I saw color. Green shoots nestled in the blackened roots. The green was scarcely visible, but it was present, growing." Looking at me again, he said, "That's when I had a really powerful sense of God drawing my attention to what I was seeing. There was the hint of promise in it. Nothing specific; no rein-statement of the dream I'd held and lost. But a definite sense that life is present. Something new is coming, and it won't be stopped."

My responses were nonverbal and, I'm sure, expressed my sense of wonder. Something as ordinary as plants among charred roots had become a means of God's grace. I admired Sam for opening his aching heart to a holy communication and appreciated the gentle presentation of love on God's part. At some point I said the word *hope*.

"Yes, hope," Sam echoed. "There is hope, but not in any particular outcome." He looked at me sternly. "I feel completely disengaged right now from the plans that had been forming in me. . . . But, yes, tentative hope. Hope that God is present. That God cares about the life that's in me. I have hope that God witnesses the scorched remains of my dream and into that devastation is bringing newness. Maybe God doesn't see the burned-out area as devastation, but sees it as beautiful in its way." I was seeing the beauty and a quiet exaltation.

"Sometimes vegetation has to burn," he continued. "Congestion of growth in a forest interferes with health, the health of the indi-vidual trees and the health of the whole forest. Maybe I needed certain things burned out of me so that what grows now is healthier," he said, tossing the thread of conversation my way with a glance.

Haunting words from the letter to the Hebrews played in my mind, unspoken: "We offer to God an acceptable worship with reverence and awe; for indeed our God is a consuming fire" (12:28-29). I nodded at the truth, ecological and theological, of what Sam said. Pruning is a real part of our spiritual lives, and it can happen in a violent way. Oliver Sachs had let go of the urgencies of his youth to open space in his old age to discover "enlargement." My parents at times spoke appreciatively of pruning (sometimes in reaction to my own not very well-pruned life) and what was possible when they let go of activities and possessions.

As I listened to Sam another image played in my mind, and I mentioned it: "I've heard there are some seeds that open and grow only when a fire releases them. I'm wondering about that in your life, Sam."

He said, "Yes, some cones of large trees only start to grow when exposed to extreme heat. That happens in forests. Maybe that happens in a person's life too. Life coming from death. Resurrection." We sat in silent reverie, prayer.

As Seeds Open

After Sam left my office, the image of a seed in which life is activated by heat stayed with me as I thought about him. Fire had immolated the dream he'd so carefully discerned and incubated. It was a dream he had cultivated over time and with prayer. There was tragedy in its loss that needed to be given its due. Yet the heat that destroyed one part of the forest of Sam's life may also have brought a vital spark to a seed that had lain dormant. Sam and I were striving to pay attention to the whole truth of his spiritual experience.

Sam said he "had a really powerful sense of God drawing my attention to what I was seeing." He opened up to the experience, giving that reality a long, loving, contemplative look. He experienced the stirring of something "new" coming, maybe even an adventure.

Shortly before she died, my mother told me she was about to embark on her "last big adventure." There would be a violent pruning, but she trusted that something new, some kind of advent, was ahead. She experienced hope as the Complete was arriving in her life, canceling her incompletes. Days before he died, Peter Ogle also wrote of what was to come—in his case, fruit in the garden. Some day we will all stand at that ultimate brink. Meanwhile, we lean toward the One who brings completion.

Every day in spiritual direction I hear people speak of the thresholds on which they stand. These people span the generations, and many of them are in seemingly stable life circumstances. Outsiders looking in on their lives would not see anything so discontinuous that it could be called a "threshold." Yet from their vantage point within their own lives, things new and unfamiliar lie ahead, just out of sight.

Sam regularly engages in the discipline of spiritual direction, which helps him attend to his experience. In my presence he re-entered the story of his hike through the burned-out wilderness and explored how it felt like a concrete representation of something he was experiencing internally. In telling me about it, he remembered the shoots of new life and felt hope being cultivated.

So, too, when I received spiritual direction after my parents' deaths, I noticed my grief and the way it existed in a larger sphere. In the experience of spaciousness—conveyed by my director's loving attention and an awareness of God's grace—I was able to experience my grief, and with that, my writing came to life. You hold it now.

May you, like Sam and the other people from around the world who are described in this book, open your heart—time and again and through the disciplines that help you do so—to God's enlivening and completing grace, that it may flow through you and bless the world.

Acknowledgments

*P*EOPLE, THEIR STORIES and their spiritual practices have helped me orient and reorient myself toward God's grace as I've worked on this book. Family members and friends have sustained me with their love and insight. With some of them I have enjoyed contact almost every day, including my beloved husband Steve, our sons Andrew and Peter, and friends Diane Deutsch and Carole Petiet. We have traveled through the thick and thin times together, and I am exceedingly grateful.

Friends and colleagues have read the book as I've been writing it, and it has benefited greatly from their questions and suggestions, though, as all authors acknowledge, responsibility for what's written here falls fully on my shoulders. Lynne Baab, Chris Corwin, Julie Lane Gay, Carole Petiet, and Steve and Andrew Phillips have been generous readers, each lending a different kind of expertise to the reading. My friend and writing partner Margret Elson has been steadfast and wise in her attention to multiple iterations of every chapter and unflagging in her encouragement of my writing over the years. I am grateful to my editor Cindy Bunch for seeking me out and inviting me to write for InterVarsity Press, as well as for the skill she has given to shaping this book.

Other people have encouraged me in ways that benefit the book, though they may not be aware of it. The community of New College

Berkeley—including Sharon Gallagher, Margaret Horwitz, Beth Henry Criss, Bonnie Howe, Peggy Alter, Ginny and Walt Hearn, Chris Corwin, Clay Radke, Rick Leong, Young-il Choo, Phil Stillman, Laurel and Ward Gasque, Lip-Bu Tan, Earl Palmer, Richard Rhodes, Pat Phillips, Janice Kamikawa, Mark Labberton, Marilyn McEntyre, Jeff Bairey, Katarina Stenstedt, Nancy Wiens, Chris Shiber, Sue Gibbons, Sarah Johnson and Jill Boyce—has been part of the soil in which I've been planted as this book has been germinating. The communities of the Graduate Theological Union, most significantly Arthur Holder and the First Presbyterian Church of Berkeley have also nourished me in my thinking and my being.

Regent College, Fuller Theological Seminary (in particular Curt Longacre) and San Francisco Theological Seminary (especially Sam Hamilton-Poore) have all given me opportunities to teach Christian spirituality and participate in the spiritual formation of students. Friends around the world have welcomed me, teaching me much about what the cultivated life looks like in different environments, and I thank them, including Atef Gendy, Father Justin Sinaites, Soohwan Park, Rudy and Shirley Rodrigues, Philip Prasad, Deepa and James Gomez, Anne Bailey, and Ivan and Sheila Satyavrata.

Other circles of community and conversation—such as a book group, a neighborhood dinner group, a women's group, a circle of prayer partners, Christian spirituality scholars and the various editorial and institutional boards on which I serve—have added seasoning to my writing, as have dear friends and relatives, including Mima Baird, Jeff Lazarus, Susan Kegeles, Bo Karen Lee, Darrah Garvin, Martha Chan, Claudia Marseille, Kathryn Muhs, Frances Reid, Sandi John, Lois Mueller, Shirley Stephenson, Evan Howard, Jean Shinoda Bolen, Carmen Neafsey, Jennie McLaurin, Luci Shaw, Mary Beaudry, Joyce French, David Sanders, Liz Smith Shonk, Krista Thigpen, Miles and Stephanie Phillips, Colin and Tina Campbell, and many others.

The people who have seen me for spiritual direction must remain unnamed here. But because our times together are long-lasting and deep, I have been able to see in these men and women the challenges confronting people of faith and also how a relationship with the living God flourishes over time and with attention. I am cultivated by their lives.

I am also grateful to people, now departed, who have blessed me and this book beyond measure. The cultivated lives of mentor-friends Mary Ann Scofield and Bob Bellah were on my mind as I wrote. Peter Ogle's reflections on his life have touched my heart, and I'm grateful for permission to quote him, a permission generously confirmed by his wife Ellen. And I acknowledge my parents Betty and Lloyd Sanders. They were daily conversation partners and friends, as well as mother and father to me, for as long as they lived. I have grown in the "significant soil" of their lives.

Appendix

GUIDELINES FOR PRACTICES

GUIDELINES FOR CONTEMPLATIVE LISTENING

This practice is the foundation for spiritual friendship and direction.
Preparation:

1. Stop and turn toward the speaker physically, mentally and spiritually.

2. Ready yourself to receive what the other person presents, and let the other person see that you are receptive.

3. Ask God to help you listen.

Awareness:

1. Notice the other with all your senses: What is communicated in words? Posture? Facial expression? Absence of words? Notice rhythms and themes as well as the progression of the narrative.

2. Notice yourself. What thoughts, feelings and sensations do you experience? Take note of them, and turn again to focusing on the speaker. Move to the background any judgments, desires to fix or your own interpretations of the speaker's experience that crop up.

3. Notice God's presence: Does the speaker refer to spiritual matters? Do you sense the Spirit in the conversation? Does what you hear resonate with God's Word? Ask God to direct your listening, and notice what most draws your attention.

Response:

1. Return repeatedly to engaged, silent attention.

2. Communicate your attunement to the other person, nonverbally (e.g., eye contact) and with verbal prompts (e.g., "Hmm").

3. Offer minimal verbal responses in a tentative way, allowing the other to correct you when you're not accurately understanding. Simply state what your attention has been drawn toward. For instance, what you've heard ("You've mentioned beauty a number of times in this story of grief"), what you've experienced while listening ("I feel moved when I hear you talk about your time at the beach") or what you notice in the speaker ("You strike me as courageous in telling this story").

4. Move with the speaker, not getting snagged on interesting details or an intriguing interpretation that comes to mind. Responsively attune yourself to the conversation as it progresses.

5. Respond with grace, imagining how the person before you is beloved by God and remembering that the speaker is vulnerable while being heard.

Closure:

1. If you bring the time to an end, do so gently and appreciatively.

2. You might let the other person know that what's been said will be held confidentially.

3. If the conversation is a mutual one and you, in turn, become the speaker, mark the transition with a moment of silence.

4. Be aware that you have received a gift. Hold the gift and its giver with respect and in prayer.

GUIDELINES FOR SABBATH LIVING

Preparation:

1. Pray about your intention to keep the sabbath holy. Read Scripture that relates to sabbath keeping (like Genesis 2:2-3, the Ten Commandments and Isaiah 58). Notice how you feel guided to hallow the day; for instance, will you keep sabbath for a few hours or for a full day, and what will mark its beginning and endpoint?

2. Put the sabbath time on your calendar. Do what you can to declutter that time of other demands and commitments. If appropriate, let people you live with know what you will be doing so that they can cooperate with your hopes.

3. Enter the time with an open heart and without an agenda.

Stopping:

1. Consciously come to a stop. Enter the sabbath with reverence and hope.

2. Allow time to help you stop (including the setting of the sun and the time on the clock).

3. Select a place for stopping (such as a garden, a chair in a quiet room or a view through a window).

4. Enlist your body in the movement of stopping (for instance, kneeling, closing your eyes, folding your hands or just sitting still).

5. Mark the beginning of the sabbath in some way, perhaps with the lighting of candles.

Turning From:

1. At least initially as you practice sabbath, try turning from the sabbath interferences mentioned in Isaiah 58.

2. Turn from work. Notice and pray about what constitutes work for you. Is gardening work or worship? Is cooking a meal for people you love work or play? Does getting some exercise make you feel joyful and free, or is it calculated or competitive?

3. Turn from social hierarchies. As with work, notice and pray about what this means for you. For example, does volunteering for a service project feel freely and happily chosen, or more like a duty or achievement? If the latter, can it be done on a day other than the sabbath? With work and hierarchy, there will be times you will interrupt your sabbath keeping for the sake of love, as is right.

4. Avoid thinking about sabbath keeping in terms of what it achieves. Sabbath is holy and for the sake of knowing God. It's not so that we can work harder during the week.

5. Notice what interferes with sabbath freedom and peace, and experiment with eliminating those obstacles from the time.

Turning Toward:

1. Set your heart to seek God. Use whatever aids you know help you do so, but don't let the aids become matters of work, pride or clutter. The invitation is to rest.

2. Notice how being alone and being with others affects your sabbath keeping. Jesus prayed with others and also went off by himself.

3. As with any relationship, we encounter the living God in the present moment. Our senses hold us in the present. Consider what sounds, sights, tastes, smells or textures open your heart.

4. Movements can also open us to the Holy. Through the centuries people have bowed, prostrated themselves, nodded their head, extended their arms, danced, walked and clapped, allowing their bodies to make a joyful noise to the Lord.

5. Words can help us turn toward God—spoken, written and sung. "He who sings prays twice" is a quotation sometimes attributed to St. Augustine and sometimes to Martin Luther. Journaling can be a helpful sabbath practice and a form of prayer.

6. Continue to notice what helps you turn toward God, for it may change.

Closure:

1. Mark the end of your sabbath. Jewish families mark the end of the sabbath with a special Havdalah service, and you might engage in a special time of prayer as the sabbath comes to a close.

2. Consider how you can express gratitude for the sabbath day and ask God's blessing on the coming week. As with the original stopping movement of sabbath, mark this occasion with time, place, posture, words, candlelight or something else that is special to you.

GUIDELINES FOR LECTIO DIVINA

These guidelines have been informed by the good work of colleagues at San Francisco Theological Seminary's Program in Christian Spirituality.

Silence. I prepare for God's address by allowing myself to experience God who is present. I shift my awareness to my senses, posture, breathing, heartbeat and God's presence.

What am I feeling right now?

Lectio. I listen to the Word, to God's address to me in these words, allowing myself to be drawn to the word or phrase that grabs, strikes, holds, calls, solicits, disturbs, resonates, pierces or stirs me in my senses, feelings, imagination or thoughts.

What word or phrase most affects me?

Meditatio. I listen again to the Word, opening myself to receive the essence of God's address to me, receiving feelings, thoughts, images and sensations that invite me into a deeper understanding of my relationships with God, myself, others, the world and nature.

What word or phrase names the feeling, thought, image, sensation or desire that stirs me?

Oratio. In silence or writing I respond to God, expressing my thoughts, feelings and desires about the meaning that has emerged for me, perhaps by giving thanks and praise, asking for help, confessing or surrendering.

I communicate with God.

Contemplatio. I wordlessly rest with God in the experience, opening my whole being to what God has stirred in me.

I silently rest with God.

Afterward. I continue to express and incarnate my experience, possibly sharing it with another person. I notice the fruit of the prayer in my life, including intentions, decisions and actions.

What would I like to express and incarnate from this experience?

GUIDELINES FOR FINDING A SPIRITUAL DIRECTOR

1. Pay attention to and pray about any particular qualities you'd want in a spiritual director (e.g., Christian, particular denomi-

national affiliation, male or female, within a certain age range, a geographical location, a particular fee range, with a certain kind of life experience, training, expertise).

2. Ask in your community about spiritual directors other people recommend, or ask at a church, a seminary or an organization that maintains a list of spiritual directors in your area. Spiritual Directors International—sdiworld.org—has a list of members, categorized by location and religious affiliation.

3. Make an initial appointment with one or more of the people you find out about, and notice how you experience the initial interactions.

4. When meeting with a spiritual director for the first time, the most important aspect to notice is what the experience is like for you. Do you feel you can trust the director? Is he or she warm and also skillful? Do you respond with hope to the director's articulation of the practice of spiritual direction? Do you resonate with the director's way of talking about God, faith and prayer? Do you feel able to explore your spiritual life in the presence of this person?

5. Other important aspects to pay attention to are more professional and may or may not matter to you: What is the director's training and ongoing supervision situation? Is the director also in spiritual direction? Does the director's presentation of the ethical aspects of the work (e.g., confidentiality, necessary reporting of dangerous situations, a focus on you rather than himself or herself, expectations about payment and scheduling) assure you of his or her competence and trustworthiness?

6. If you find a spiritual director with whom you feel comfortable, after a number of meetings review the experience. Pray and pay

attention to how the work contributes to your desire to open your heart more and more to God. Spiritual direction is primarily about your relationship with God, not your relationship with the director, so notice what's happening in your spiritual life as a result of, or in conjunction with, the direction work. You might want to journal about this, talk it over with a spiritual friend and also discuss it with the director.

If you find the work with this spiritual director is not helpful, feel free to let the person know and return to looking for a director who is a better match for you. If the work is helpful, continue with it for as long as you desire. There's no expected end to the work of spiritual direction. As long as we are cultivating our lives by God's grace, this is a discipline that can aid in that.

GUIDELINES FOR CULTIVATING FRIENDSHIP

1. *Receiving.* Friends receive friends. A friend is a welcome part of our life, including our thoughts, history, feelings and soul. We make room in our life and heart for a friend and receive a friend's welcome.

2. *Trusting self-disclosure.* We trust a friend. When we speak, we try to be emotionally honest, knowing there are privacy constraints even in soul friendship (e.g., confidences from the home or the workplace). In a spiritual friendship, we speak about our relationship with God and how that affects our life.

3. *Communicated empathy.* When a friend speaks to us with trust, we open our heart, letting the friend know that we care and register the friend's feelings. The practice of "contemplative listening" is an excellent way of communicating empathy. This practice helps us steer clear of problem solving, advice giving,

judgment and scene stealing, so that we can help a friend go deeper into self-awareness and God-awareness.

4. *Cultivated insight, personal and cultural.* We are receptive to what's reflected in the mirror that our friend is to us. Listening to a friend's response is a way of growing in knowledge about our self, the world and God.

5. *Called by name.* We remind a friend of who he or she is, namely, a person God calls "beloved." With kindness and honesty, we encourage and, sometimes, challenge a friend.

6. *Accompaniment through thick and thin.* We love a friend through all kinds of seasons, even final ones, as best we can and by God's grace. We notice what our friend is experiencing and are present for him or her, even as we bring our own feelings into our awareness before God. In spiritual friendship, we seek the grace to confess and forgive.

7. *Celebration.* Spiritual friends rejoice together and are thankful for the gift of friendship. Celebration should be a core practice of friendship, as it is in family life, nations and the church.

NOTES

FOREWORD

[1] Eugen Rosenstock-Huessy's work is described in George Allen Morgan's *Speech and Society: The Christian Linguistic Social Philosophy of Eugen Rosenstock-Huessy* (Gainesville, FL: University Presses of Florida, 1987), p. 5.

INTRODUCTION: LEAVING THE CIRCUS

[1] Katherine Boo, *Behind the Beautiful Forevers* (New York: Random House, 2012), pp. 198-99.

[2] Ibid.

[3] Ibid., pp. 218, 220, 241.

[4] George Lakoff and Mark Johnson, *Philosophy in the Flesh: The Embodied Mind and Its Challenge to Western Thought* (New York: Basic Books, 1999), p. 47.

[5] Ibid., p. 567.

[6] Part of the Rural Presbyterian Church–India, founded by Philip Prasad and others.

[7] Sathianathan Clarke, Deenabandhu Manchala and Philip Vinod Peacock, "Introduction: Enflamed Words, Engaging Worlds, Embryonic Word-Worlds," in *Dalit Theology in the Twenty-First Century: Discordant Voices, Discerning Pathways,* ed. Sathianathan Clarke, Deenabandhu Manchala and Philip Vinod Peacock (New York: Oxford University Press, 2010), p. 13.

[8] Em Griffin, *A First Look at Communication Theory,* 7th ed. (Boston: McGraw-Hill Higher Education, 2009), p. 349.

[9] See www.med.umich.edu/yourchild/topics/tv.htm, 2010.

[10] The article I wrote from the seminar given at the Oxford Centre for Mission Studies, which has influenced this book, is "Garden or Circus? Christian Care in the Face of Contemporary Pressures," *Transformation: An International Dialogue on Mission and Ethics* 22, no. 3 (July 2005): 158-65 (all material from

that article that is quoted in this book is used by permission of the journal).

[11]Christian Wiman, *My Bright Abyss: Meditation of a Modern Believer* (New York: Farrar, Straus and Giroux, 2013), p. 85.

[12]Michael Luo, "Immigrants Hear God's Word in Chinese, via Conference Call," *New York Times,* May 21, 2006, p. 1.

[13]Ibid., p. 31.

[14]William James, *Talks to Teachers on Psychology: And to Students on Some of Life's Ideals* (1899; Rockville, MD: Arc Manor, 2008), p. 57.

CHAPTER ONE: THE WAY OF CULTIVATION

[1]The Book of Common Prayer is available at www.bcponline.org.

[2]In the Greek the words are *peripateite, errizōmenoi.*

[3]See, for example, Erik H. Erikson, *Identity and the Life Cycle* (New York: International Universities Press, 1959).

[4]Bronnie Ware, "Top 5 Regrets of the Dying," *Huff Post, The Blog,* January 21, 2012, www.huffingtonpost.com/bronnie-ware/top-5-regrets-of-the-dyin_b_1220965.html.

[5]John Calvin, *New Testament Commentaries*, trans. T. H. L. Parker (1555; Grand Rapids: Eerdmans, 1972), 11:183, on Ephesians 4:14, quoted by William J. Bouwsma, "Christian Adulthood," in *Adulthood*, ed. Erik H. Erikson (New York: W. W. Norton, 1978), p. 85.

[6]Karl Barth, letter of December 31, 1958, cited in *The Christian Century Reader: Representative Articles, Editorials, and Poems*, ed. Harold E. Fey and Margaret Frakes (New York: Association Press, 1962), pp. 102-5.

[7]T. S. Eliot, "The Dry Salvages," in *Four Quartets* (San Diego: Harcourt Brace, 1943), l. 214.

[8]See, for example, Proverbs 4:14, which warns against walking on "the way of evildoers."

[9]Psalm 1:3. "Blessed" here in Hebrew is *ashrei.* The word is a cognate of the verb meaning "going straight," which in Hebrew is *asher.*

[10]Augustine of Hippo, Sermon 189.4, quoted by Lawrence S. Cunningham, "The Way and the Ways," in *Life in the Spirit: Spiritual Formation in Theological Perspective,* ed. Jeffrey P. Greenman and George Kalantzis (Downers Grove, IL: IVP Academic, 2010), p. 85.

[11]Harvey Cox, *The Future of Faith* (New York: HarperOne, 2009), p. 10.

[12]The book of Acts uses the word *Hodou* in 9:2 and later.

[13]Gustavo Gutiérrez, *We Drink from Our Own Wells: The Spiritual Journey of*

a People, trans. Matthew J. O'Connell (New York: Orbis Books, 1985), p. 81.

[14]T. S. Eliot, "Choruses from *The Rock,*" in *Collected Poems: 1909-1935* (New York: Harcourt, Brace, 1936), p. 179, sec. 1, l. 14.

CHAPTER TWO: FINDING AND RECEIVING REFRESHMENT

[1]For instance, see Sandra Schneiders, "The Study of Christian Spirituality: Contours and Dynamics," in *Minding the Spirit: The Study of Christian Spirituality,* ed. Elizabeth A. Dreyer and Mark S. Burrows (Baltimore: Johns Hopkins University Press, 2005), pp. 5-24.

[2]Belden C. Lane, *The Solace of Fierce Landscapes: Exploring Desert and Mountain Spirituality* (New York: Oxford University Press, 1998).

[3]*The Ogler,* http://theogler.blogspot.com.

[4]April 22, 2013, personal communication.

[5]*Online Etymology Dictionary,* s.v. "carpe diem," www.etymonline.com/.

[6]*The Ogler,* May 2, 2013, as dictated to his daughter and son, Allison and Nick.

[7]Elizabeth Goudge, *The Little White Horse* (London: Puffin Books, 1974), p. 136.

[8]Janet Martin Soskice, *Metaphor and Religious Language* (Oxford: Clarendon, 1985), p. 160.

CHAPTER THREE: LISTENING AS A WAY OF RECEIVING CULTIVATION

[1]Simone Weil, *Gravity and Grace* (London: Routledge, 1952), p. 105.

[2]Karl Rahner, *The Need and Blessing of Prayer,* trans. Bruce W. Gillette (Collegeville, MN: Liturgical, 1997), p. 1.

[3]See the work of Roy Baumeister and his colleagues on ego depletion; e.g. Roy F. Baumeister, Ellen Bratslavsky, Mark Murraven and Diane M. Tice, "Ego Depletion: Is the Active Ego a Limited Resource?," *Journal of Personality and Social Structure* 74, no. 5 (1998): 1252-65.

[4]Teddy Wayne, "Call Waiting . . . and Waiting," *New York Times,* January 5, 2014, sec. ST, p. 2.

[5]Charles Taylor, "The Politics of Recognition," in *Multiculturalism: Examining the Politics of Recognition,* ed. Amy Guttmann (Princeton, NJ: Princeton University Press, 1994), p. 24.

[6]Most notably, the philosopher Michel Foucault.

[7]For instance, see the work of the sociologist Erving Goffman.

[8]W. B. Yeats [1893], *The Celtic Twilight* (Gerrards Cross, UK: Colin Smythe, 1981), p. 100.

[9]Dietrich Bonhoeffer, *Life Together*, trans. John W. Doberstein (1938; New York: Harper and Row, 1954), p. 97.

[10]E.g., Ephesians 5:1.

[11]Marjorie O'Rourke Boyle, "*Sermo*: Reopening the Conversation on Translating JN 1,1," *Vigiliae Christianae* 31, no. 3 (September 1977): 161-68.

[12]Martin Buber, *The Way of Response: Martin Buber—Selections from His Writings*, ed. N. N. Glatzer (New York: Schocken Books, 1966), p. 38— evoking Moses' words in Deuteronomy 4:12.

[13]Paul Carter, "Ambiguous Traces, Mishearing, and Auditory Space," in *Hearing Cultures: Essays on Sounds, Listening and Modernity*, ed. Veit Erlmann (Oxford: Berg, 2004), p. 43.

[14]Listening is hearing toward or for, as illuminated by the German *hören*, to hear, and *zuhören*, to listen (the prefix *zu-* meaning to, at, in, on or by).

[15]See Martin Heidegger, "Logos (Heraclitus, Fragment B 50)", in *Early Greek Thinking*, trans. David Farrell Krell and Frank A. Capuzzi (1954; New York: Harper and Row, 1975), pp. 59-78.

[16]Michel Foucault, "Pastoral Power and Political Reason", in *Religion and Culture: Michel Foucault*, ed. Jeremy R. Carrette (1979; New York: Routledge, 1999), p. 138.

[17]Heidegger, "Logos," p. 78.

[18]Hans-Georg Gadamer, *Truth and Method*, 2nd rev. ed., trans. and rev. Joel Weinsheimer and Donald G. Marshall (New York: Crossroad, 1989), p. 361.

[19]Heraclitus, Fragment 19, www.archimedes-lab.org/heraclitus_aphorism .html.

[20]Helen Epstein, "Talking Their Way Out of a Population Crisis," *New York Times*, October 23, 2011, p. SR4.

CHAPTER FOUR: STOPPING

[1]Mary Oliver, "Wild Geese," available at www.phys.unm.edu/~tw/fas/yits /archive/oliver_wildgeese.html.

[2]Peggy Orenstein, "Stop Your Search Engines: Forcing Ourselves Offline May Be the Path to True Knowledge," *New York Times Magazine*, October 25, 2009, pp. 11-12.

[3]James Kugel, *In the Valley of the Shadow: On the Foundations of Religious Belief* (New York: Free Press, 2011), p. 86.

[4]Josef Pieper, *Leisure: The Basis of Culture, including "The Philosophical Act,"* trans. Alexander Dru (1952; San Francisco: Ignatius, 2009), p. 46.

[5]Quoted by Susie Linfield, "Trading Truth for Justice? Reflections on South Africa's Truth and Reconciliation Commission," *Boston Review,* Summer 2000, http://bostonreview.net/world/susie-linfield-trading-truth-justice.

[6]See Lawrence W. Sherman and Heather Strang, *Restorative Justice: The Evidence* (Philadelphia: University of Pennsylvania, 2007).

[7]Peter Storey, "A Different Kind of Justice: Truth and Reconciliation in South Africa," *New World Outlook,* July-August 1999, excerpted from *Christian Century,* September 10-17, 1997.

[8]Hans-Georg Gadamer, *Truth and Method,* 2nd rev. ed., trans. and rev. Joel Weinsheimer and Donald G. Marshall (New York: Crossroad, 1989), p. 361.

[9]Walter J. Burghardt, "Contemplation: A Long, Loving Look at the Real," *Church,* Winter 1989, pp. 14-18.

[10]Linfield, "Trading Truth for Justice?" Specifically, she cites the work of Theodor Adorno, a German philosopher who urged Germany to take time to acknowledge the suffering it had inflicted during the Holocaust.

[11]See John Borneman, *Political Crime and the Memory of Loss* (Bloomington: Indiana University Press, 2011), especially chap. 4, "Reconciliation After Ethnic Cleansing: Listening, Retribution, Affiliation."

CHAPTER FIVE: SABBATH KEEPING

[1]See, for example, Eugene H. Peterson, *Christ Plays in Ten Thousand Places: A Conversation in Spiritual Theology* (London: Hodder and Stoughton, 2005), p. 109.

[2]Material has been used, with permission of the journal, from my article "Stop in the Name of Love! The Radical Practice of Sabbath-Keeping," *Crux: A Quarterly Journal of Christian Thought and Opinion* 47, no. 3 (Fall 2011): 2-13.

[3]See Laura Vanderkam, "Overestimating Our Overworking," *Wall Street Journal,* May 29, 2009, p. W13.

[4]Josef Pieper, *Leisure: The Basis of Culture, Including The Philosophical Act,* trans. Alexander Dru (1952; San Francisco: Ignatius, 2009), p. 46.

[5]Pico Iyer, "The Joy of Quiet," *New York Times,* January 1, 2012, p. SR1.

[6]Mark Oppenheimer, "Pope Francis Has a Few Words in Support of Leisure," *New York Times,* April 26, 2013, www.nytimes.com/2013/04/27/us/pope-francis-has-a-few-words-in-support-of-leisure.html.

[7]Letter of May 22, 1709, in *Susanna Wesley: The Complete Writings,* ed. Charles Wallace Jr. (Oxford: Oxford University Press, 1997), p. 304.

[8]Ibid.

[9]The Shabbat blessing is quoted in Lynne M. Baab, *Sabbath Keeping: Finding Freedom in the Rhythms of Rest* (Downers Grove, IL: InterVarsity Press, 2005), p. 127.

[10]Abraham Joshua Heschel, *The Sabbath: Its Meaning for Modern Man* (Boston: Shambala, 2003), p. 93.

[11]See Charles Taylor, *A Secular Age* (Cambridge, MA: Belknap Press of Harvard University Press, 2007), p. 54.

[12]Ibid., pp. 56-57.

[13]Heschel, *Sabbath,* p. xv.

[14]Eugene Peterson, "Confessions of a Former Sabbath Breaker," *Christianity Today,* September 2, 1988, p. 26.

[15]See Juvenal, Seneca and others.

[16]Such as Philo.

[17]Aristotle, *Nicomachean Ethics* 10.6.34-35.

[18]William Shakespeare, *Macbeth,* act 2, scene 2, lines 37-40.

[19]Mark 2:23-28; 3:1-6; Luke 14:1-6; John 5:1-18; 9:1-41, cited by Peterson, *Christ Plays in Ten Thousand Places,* p. 112.

[20]Ben and Carol Weir, with Dennis Benson, *Hostage Bound, Hostage Free* (Philadelphia: Westminster Press, 1987), p. 51.

[21]Ibid., pp. 51-52.

[22]Ibid., p. 52.

[23]Ibid.

CHAPTER SIX: CULTIVATING ATTENTION

[1]See Amir Raz and Jason Buhle, "Typologies of Attentional Networks," *Nature: Nature Reviews / Neuroscience* 7 (May 2006): 367-79.

[2]Kate Pickert, "The Art of Being Mindful," *Time,* February 3, 2014, p. 42.

[3]See, for example, Han de Wit, "The Case for Contemplative Psychology," *Shambala Sun,* March 2001, www.bemindful.org/contemppsychart.pdf.

[4]Italics in original. Susan Abraham, "Purifying Memory and Dispossessing the Self: Spiritual Strategies in the Postcolonial Classroom," *Spiritus* 13, no. 1 (Spring 2013): 70.

[5]Jon Kabat-Zinn, "Mindfulness-Based Interventions in Context: Past, Present, and Future," *Clinical Psychology: Science and Practice* 10, no. 2 (2003): 145.

[6]Hooria Jazaieri and Shauna L. Shapiro, "Managing Stress Mindfully," in *Contemplative Practices in Action: Spirituality, Meditation, and Health,* ed. Thomas G. Plante (Santa Barbara, CA: Praeger, 2010), p. 17.

[7]Personal notes from a conference with Jon Kabat-Zinn, "The Science of a Meaningful Life: Practicing Mindfulness and Compassion," Richmond, CA, March 8, 2013.

[8]Pickert, "Art of Being Mindful," pp. 42-46.

[9]Stephen P. Stratton, "Mindfulness and Contemplation: Secular and Religious Traditions in Western Context," unpublished manuscript, p. 3.

[10]Italics used in the original. Kirk Warren Brown, Richard M. Ryan and J. David Creswell, "Mindfulness: Theoretical Foundations and Evidence for Its Salutary Effects," *Psychological Inquiry: An International Journal for the Advancement of Psychological Theory* 18, no. 4 (2007): 212.

[11]Liz Kulze, "How Meditation Works," *Atlantic,* June 27, 2013, www.the atlantic.com/health/archive/2013/06/how-meditation-works/277275/.

[12]See, for example, Eleanor Rosch, "The Grinch Who Stole Wisdom," in *The Scientific Study of Personal Wisdom: From Contemplative Traditions to Neuroscience,* ed. Michael Ferrari and Nic M. Westrate (Amsterdam: Springer, 2013), pp. 229-49.

[13]Fran Lowry, "Wide Global Variation in ADHD Diagnosis and Treatment," *Medscape,* May 5, 2011, www.medscape.com/viewarticle/742133. The article disputes wide global variation in prevalence and diagnosis, while discussing variation in treatment.

[14]The new *Diagnostic and Statistical Manual* of the American Psychiatric Association (*DSM-5,* 2013) makes it easier for clinicians to diagnose the disorder in teens and adults.

[15]Alan Schwartz, "The Selling of Attention Deficit Disorder: The Number of Diagnoses Soared amid a 20-Year Drug Marketing Campaign," *New York Times,* December 15, 2013, pp. 1, 26-27.

[16]Winston Chung, "Be Sure It's ADHD Before You Medicate," *San Francisco Chronicle,* May 1, 2013, pp. D1, D4.

[17]Lowry, "Wide Global Variation."

[18]See Vatsal G. Thakkar, "Diagnosing the Wrong Deficit: Could What Looks Like A.D.H.D. Be a Sleep Disorder in Disguise?," *New York Times,* April 28, 2013, pp. SR1, SR6.

[19]See Judith Shulevitz, "The Lethality of Loneliness: We Now Know How It Can Ravage Our Body and Brain," *New Republic,* May 13, 2013, p. 7.

[20]Robert N. Bellah, "Understanding Caring in Contemporary America," in *The Crisis of Care: Affirming and Restoring Caring Practices in the Helping Professions,* ed. Susan S. Phillips and Patricia Benner (Wash-

ington, DC: Georgetown University Press, 1994), p. 28.

[21]See Michel Foucault, "About the Beginning of the Hermeneutics of the Self (1980)," in *Religion and Culture,* ed. Jeremy R. Carrette (New York: Routledge, 1999), p. 166.

[22]Peter Ochs, "Morning Prayer as Redemptive Thinking," in *Liturgy, Time and the Politics of Redemption,* ed. Randi Rashover and C. C. Pecknold (Grand Rapids: Eerdmans, 2006), p. 61.

[23]Ibid., p. 81.

CHAPTER SEVEN: PRAYING WITH SCRIPTURE

[1]See, for example, Laurel S. Gasque, "The Bible of the Poor: An Example of Medieval Interpretation and Its Relevance Today," in *Imagination and Interpretation: Christian Perspectives,* ed. Hans Boersma (Vancouver, BC: Regent College Publishing, 2005), pp. 57-67. This entire book addresses imaginative ways of interpreting (and praying with) Scripture.

[2]There are helpful books available on the practice of lectio divina, and I have benefited from many of them, including Michael Casey, *Sacred Reading: The Ancient Art of Lectio Divina* (Ligouri, MO: Triumph Books, 1995); Charles Dumont, *Praying the Word of God: The Use of Lectio Divina* (Fairacres, Oxford: SLG Press, 1999); John C. Endres and Elizabeth Liebert, *A Retreat with the Psalms: Resources for Personal and Communal Prayer* (New York: Paulist, 2001); Thelma Hall, *Too Deep for Words: Rediscovering Lectio Divina* (New York: Paulist, 1988); Evan Howard, *Praying the Scriptures: A Field Guide for Your Spiritual Journey* (Downers Grove, IL: InterVarsity Press, 1999); Robert J. Miller, *Falling into Faith: Lectio Divina Series* (Franklin, WI: Sheed and Ward, 2000); Basil M. Pennington, *Lectio Divina* (New York: Crossroad, 1998); and James C. Wilhoit and Evan Howard, *Discovering Lectio Divina: Bringing Scripture into Ordinary Life* (Downers Grove, IL: InterVarsity Press, 2012).

[3]Kathleen Norris, *Cloister Walk* (New York: Riverhead Books, 1996), pp. 102-3.

[4]In the *Scala claustralium* (ladder of ascent): Guigo II [12th century], *Lettre sur la vie contemplative,* chaps. 2-7, Sources chretiennes 163, ed. Edmund Colledge and James Walsh, no. 163 (Paris: Editions du Cerf, 1970), pp. 83-97.

[5]Quoted by Charles Dumont, *Praying the Word of God: The Use of Lectio Divina* (Oxford: Fairacres, 1999), p. 13.

[6]Brief Rule of the Camaldolese Order, www.camaldolese.com/information .html, accessed October 15, 2013.

[7]Geoff New, "Third Things First: Preaching and Ignatian Contemplation," *The Way: A Review of Christian Spirituality* 52, no. 4 (October 2013): 83-93.

[8]See the work of Timothy Wilson and his colleagues at the University of Virginia and Harvard University, for example, summarized in "Doing Something Is Better Than Doing Nothing for Most People, Study Shows," press release, EurekAlert!, July 3, 2014, www.eurekalert.org/pub_releases/2014-07/uov-dsi063014.php.

CHAPTER EIGHT: CULTIVATING ATTACHMENT

[1]Abraham Joshua Heschel, "No Time for Neutrality," in *Moral Grandeur and Spiritual Audacity*, ed. Susannah Heschel (New York: Farrar, Straus and Giroux, 1996), p. 112.

[2]Starfishncoffeeelephantsnflower's response, quoted in Derek Thompson, "No-Vacation Nation: 'As Long as There's WiFi . . . I Am on the Clock,'" *Atlantic,* August 7, 2012, www.theatlantic.com/business/print/2012/08/no-vacation-nation-as-long-as-theres-wifi-i-am-on-the-clock/260804. Original article: Derek Thompson, "The Only Advanced Country Without a National Vacation Policy? It's the US," *Atlantic,* July 2, 2012.

[3]John Cassian, *The Institutes* 10.2, trans. Boniface Ramsey (2000), quoted in Stephen Greenblatt, *The Swerve: How the World Became Modern* (New York: W. W. Norton, 2011), p. 26.

[4]See, for example, the study of screen time and empathy among more than two thousand adolescents in seven countries: Sara Prot et al., "Long-Term Relations Among Prosocial-Media Use, Empathy and Prosocial Behavior," abstract, *Psychological Science,* December 11, 2013, http://pss.sagepub.com/content/early/2013/12/11/0956797613503854.abstract?papetoc.

[5]See Amir Levine and Rachel Heller, *Attached: The New Science of Adult Attachment and How It Can Help You Find—and Keep—Love* (New York: Jeremy Tarcher, 2010).

[6]"In Praise of Misfits: Why Business Needs People with Asperger's Syndrome, Attention-Deficit Disorder and Dyslexia," Schumpeter blog, *Economist,* June 2, 2012, www.economist.com/node/21556230.

[7]Judith Shulevitz, "The Lethality of Loneliness: We Now Know How It Can Ravage Our Body and Brain," *New Republic,* May 13, 2013), www.newrepublic.com/node/113176.

[8]Ilene Philipson, "Work Is Life: A Psychologist Looks at Identity and Work

in America," Psychotherapy.net, 2001, www.psychotherapy.net/article /work-is-life.

[9]Ibid.

[10]See, for example, Phillip R. Shaver, Shiri Lavy, Clifford D. Saron, and Mario Mikulincer, "Social Foundations of the Capacity for Mindfulness: An Attachment Perspective," *Psychological Inquiry* 18, no. 4 (2007): 264-71.

[11]W. H. Auden, "September 1, 1939," available at Poem du Jour, www.poem dujour.com/Sept1.1939.html, and David J. Wallin, *Attachment in Psychotherapy* (New York: Guilford Press, 2007).

[12]See, for example, Frank Newport, Dan Witters and Sangeeta Agrawal, "Religious Americans Enjoy Higher Wellbeing," Gallup, www.gallup.com /poll/152723/religious-americans-enjoy-higher-wellbeing-aspx. See also Matthew T. Lee, Margaret M. Poloma and Stephen G. Post, *The Heart of Religion: Spiritual Empowerment, Benevolence, and the Experience of God's Love* (New York: Oxford University Press, 2013).

[13]Barbara Ehrenreich, *Bright-Sided: How the Relentless Promotion of Positive Thinking Has Undermined America* (New York: Metropolitan Books, 2009), p. 146.

[14]Jalal al-Din Rumi, "A Community of the Spirit," in *The Essential Rumi*, new exp. ed., trans. Coleman Barks (New York: HarperOne, 2004), p. 3.

[15]Sigmund Freud, "Recommendations to Physicians Practicing Psychoanalysis" in *Standard Edition* (1912; London: Hogarth, 1958), 7:109-20.

[16]Julian of Norwich, *Revelations of Divine Love* (14th century), trans. Father John-Julian (Brewster, MA: Paraclete, 2011), p. 64.

[17]Belden C. Lane, *The Solace of Fierce Landscapes: Exploring Desert and Mountain Spirituality* (New York: Oxford University Press, 2007), p. 191.

[18]Barna research cited in Bruce Demarest, *Four Views on Christian Spirituality* (Grand Rapids: Zondervan, 2012), p. 16.

[19]Peter Ogle, "The Ogler," February 4, 2012.

Chapter Nine: Spiritual Direction

[1]For my extended reflections on spiritual direction, see my book *Candlelight: Illuminating the Art of Spiritual Direction* (Harrisburg, PA: Morehouse, 2008).

[2]More ideas about the significance of story can be found in my article "Telling Our Stories: Spiritual Direction, Healing Gift," *Conversations: A Forum for Authentic Transformation* 10, no. 2 (Fall/Winter 2012): 34-38.

[3]More on this topic can be found in a chapter I wrote: "Spiritual Direction as a Navigational Aid in Sanctification," in *Life in the Spirit: Spiritual Formation in Theological Perspective,* ed. Jeffrey P. Greenman and George Kalantzis (Downers Grove, IL: IVP Academic, 2010), pp. 160-79.

[4]John Climacus, quoted in Kallistos Ware, "Foreword: The Spiritual Father in Saint John Climacus and Saint Symeon the New Theologian," in Irenee Hausherr, *Spiritual Direction in the Early Christian East,* trans. Anthony P. Gythiel (Kalamazoo, MI: Cistercian, 1990), p. xxvii.

[5]Kallistos Ware, introduction to John Climacus, *The Ladder of Divine Ascent,* trans. Cilm Lubheid and Norman Russell (Mahwah, NJ: Paulist, 1982), p. 37.

[6]See James M. May, "Love of Wisdom the Guide of Life," address to the Phi Beta Kappa Society of St. Olaf College, April 24, 2003, http://wp.stolaf.edu /pbk/index-6/james_m_may/.

[7]Gregory Boyle, *Tattoos on the Heart: The Power of Boundless Compassion* (New York: Free Press, 2010).

[8]Ibid., p. 23.

[9]Ibid., pp. 22-23.

[10]Ibid., p. 23.

[11]Ibid.

[12]Ibid., p. 24.

[13]Ibid.

[14]Ibid.

CHAPTER TEN: ROOTED AND GROUNDED BY FRIENDSHIP

[1]Peter Ogle, *The Ogler,* April 3, 2013.

[2]Ibid., April 9, 2013.

[3]Bronnie Ware, "Top 5 Regrets of the Dying," *The Blog, HuffPost,* January 21, 2012, www.huffingtonpost.com/bronnie-ware/top-5-regrets-of-the-dyin_b _1220965.html.

[4]The statement is quoted frequently, but its origin is elusive. See, for instance, www.oakparkjournal.com/TheaterReviews/2011-OakParkFestivalTheatre -The-Glass-Menagerie.html.

[5]Jacques Derrida's *The Politics of Friendship,* trans. George Collins (London: Verso, 1997), is an extended reflection on this statement.

[6]See Aristotle, *Nicomachean Ethics* (4th c. B.C.), trans. Martin Ostwald (Indianapolis: Bobbs-Merrill Educational, 1962), bk. 8.

[7]Aelred of Rievaulx, *Spiritual Friendship* (A.D. 1164-67), trans. Mary Eugenia Laker (Kalamazoo, MI: Cistercian, 1977).

[8]Milan Kundera, *Encounter,* trans. Linda Asher (New York: HarperCollins, 2010), p. 114.

[9]Jane Conrad and Marilyn Lovell, "Space and Time: A Talk with Two of the Women Behind America's First Astronauts," interview by Connie Schultz, *Parade,* July 2, 2013, p. 14.

[10]C. S. Lewis, *The Four Loves* (New York: Collins, 1974), p. 69.

[11]John Von Heyking and Richard Avramenko, introduction to *Friendship and Politics: Essays in Political Thought,* ed. Von Heyking and Avramenko (Notre Dame, IN: University of Notre Dame Press, 2008), p. 3.

[12]Lewis, *Four Loves,* p. 71.

[13]Kate Taylor, "She Can Play That Game, Too," *New York Times,* July 14, 2013, sec. ST, p. 6.

[14]See Michael Pakaluk, ed., *Other Selves: Philosophers on Friendship* (Indianapolis: Hackett, 1991), p. 111, quoting Cicero, *On Friendship (De Amicitia)* (44 B.C.), trans. Frank Copley (Ann Arbor: University of Michigan Press, 1967).

[15]See Aristotle's *Nicomachean Ethics*—many editions are available, including *Introduction to Aristotle* by Richard McKeon (Chicago: University of Chicago Press, 1973), 332-581; Cicero, "Laelius, or An Essay on Friendship," in *Cicero's Offices with Laelius, Cato Maior and Select Letters* (London: J. M. Dent and Sons, 1966), pp. 167-215; Aelred of Rievaulx, *Spiritual Friendship*; Søren Kierkegaard, *Works of Love,* trans. Howard and Edna Hong (New York: Harper and Row, 1964); Anders Nygren, *Agape and Eros,* trans. Philip S. Watson (New York: Harper and Row, 1969).

[16]See, for example, Jon Gertner's "The Rise and Fall of the G.D.P.," *New York Times Magazine,* May 16, 2010, pp. 60-71.

[17]See, for example, Nicholas Carr, *The Shallows: What the Internet Is Doing to Our Brains* (New York: W. W. Norton, 2010), and Robert D. Putnam, *Bowling Alone: The Collapse and Revival of American Community* (New York: Simon and Schuster, 2000).

[18]The research of Sara Konrath, quoted by Pamela Paul, "From Students, Less Kindness for Strangers?," *New York Times,* June 27, 2010, p. S5.

[19]Lynne Baab, "The Future Church: Identity and Persuasion on Congregational Websites" (PhD diss., University of Washington, 2007), p. 188. Accessible at www.lynnebaab.com/academic. (Baab was drawing on circus imagery from my article "Garden or Circus? Christian Care in the Face of

Contemporary Pressures," *Transformation: An International Dialogue on Mission and Ethics* 22, no. 3 (July 2005): 158-65.

[20]See, for example, Hilary Stout's article "A Best Friend? You Must Be Kidding?," *New York Times,* June 16, 2010, www.nytimes.com/2010/06/17 /fashion/17BFF.html?pagewanted=all&_r=0.

[21]Number of users at the time this was written in August 2014, up from 400 million in June 2010: http://newsroom.fb.com/company-info.

[22]Aaron Smith, "6 New Facts About Facebook," Pew Research Center, February 3, 2014, www.pewresearch.org/fact-tank/2014/02/03/6-new-facts -about-facebook.

[23]Paul Adams, "Designing for Social Interaction: Strong, Weak, and Temporary Interactions," *Boxes and Arrows,* April 9, 2010, www.boxesandarrows .com/view/designing-for-social.

[24]See, for example, the work of British anthropologists Robin Durbar, Nichola Christakis and James Fowler, *Connected: The Surprising Power of Our Social Networks and How They Shape Our Lives* (New York: Little, Brown, 2009), cited in ibid.

[25]"Faithful friends are a sturdy shelter: whoever finds one has found a treasure" (Sirach 6:14).

CHAPTER ELEVEN: PRACTICING FRIENDSHIP

[1]"By the Book: Amy Bloom," *New York Times Book Review,* August 3, 2014, p. 8, referring to James Marshall's book *George and Martha* (New York: HMH Books for Young Readers, 1974).

[2]John O'Donahue, *Anam Cara: A Book of Celtic Wisdom* (San Francisco: Harper Perennial, 1998).

[3]Lynne M. Baab, *Friending: Real Relationships in a Virtual World* (Downers Grove, IL: InterVarsity Press, 2011), p. 14.

[4]Dallas Willard, *The Spirit of the Disciplines: Understanding How God Changes Lives* (San Francisco: HarperSanFrancisco, 1988), p. ix.

[5]See Douglas Harper, *Online Etymology Dictionary,* s.v. "friend," www.etym online.com/index.php?search=friend&searchmode=none. See also Lothar Krappman, "Amicitia, drujba, shin-yu, philia, freundschaft, friendship: On the cultural diversity of a human relationship," in *The Company They Keep: Friendship in Childhood and Adolescence,* ed. William M. Bukowski, Andrew F. Newcomb and Willard W. Hartup (Cambridge: Cambridge Univ. Press, 1996), p. 23.

[6]"Introduction: The Persistence of Friendship in Political Life" in *Friendship and Politics: Essays in Political Thought*, ed. John Von Heyking and Richard Avramenko (Notre Dame, IN: University of Notre Dame Press, 2008), p. 3.

[7]Catherine M. Wallace, *For Fidelity: How Intimacy and Commitment Enrich Our Lives* (New York: Alfred A. Knopf, 1998), p. 112.

[8]See Diana Walsh's article "Children Learning Game of Friendship," *San Francisco Chronicle*, April 14, 2002, pp. A21, A23.

[9]Emily Dickinson, "Poem #303" (ca. 1862), in *The Complete Poems of Emily Dickinson*, ed. Thomas H. Johnson (Boston: Little, Brown, 1960), p. 143.

[10]Madeleine L'Engle and Luci Shaw, *Friends for the Journey* (Ann Arbor, MI: Servant, 1997), p. 145.

[11]See, for instance, Lyman Wynne and Adele Wynne, "The Quest for Intimacy," *Journal of Marital and Family Therapy* 12, no. 4 (October 1986): 383-94.

[12]Henri J. M. Nouwen, *Out of Solitude: Three Meditations on the Christian Life* (Notre Dame, IN: Ave Maria, 2004), p. 38.

[13]Bronnie Ware, "Top 5 Regrets of the Dying," *The Blog, HuffPost,* January 21, 2012, www.huffingtonpost.com/bronnie-ware/top-5-regrets-of-the-dyin_b_1220965.html.

CHAPTER TWELVE: BEARING FRUIT AND
ENRICHING THE SOIL

[1]Jeanne Guyon, *A Short and Very Easy Method of Prayer,* trans. T. D. Brook (New York: Cosimo Classics, 2007), p. 65; referenced by Bo Karen Lee, "Madame Jeanne Guyon (1648-1717): A Short and Very Easy Method of Prayer," in *Christian Spirituality: The Classics*, ed. Arthur Holder (London: Routledge, 2009), pp. 257-67.

[2]See, for example, Douglas F. Kelly's "The Westminster Shorter Catechism," in *To Glorify and Enjoy God: A Commemoration of the 350th Anniversary of the Westminster Assembly,* ed. John L. Carlson and David W. Hall (Edinburgh: Banner of Truth Trust, 1994).

[3]Michelle Faul, "Man Survives 3 Days at Bottom of Atlantic," Philly.com, December 3, 2013, www.twincities.com/olympics/ci_24645377/man-survives-60-hours-at-bottom-atlantic.

[4]Associated Press, "Rescue Diver Almost Missed Capsized Boat's Survivor," *San Francisco Chronicle,* December 12, 2013, p. A7. The YouTube video, *Har-*

rison Okene Rescued After 3 Days Under Water in Shipwreck, is available at www.youtube.com/watch?v=ZPz8mxJNPh8.

[5]Jonathan Haidt, "Elevation and the Positive Psychology of Morality," in *Flourishing: Positive Psychology and the Well-Lived Life,* ed. Corey L. M. Keyes and Jonathan Haidt (Washington, DC: American Psychological Association 2003), p. 276.

[6]Widely available, including at www.shakespeare-online.com/sonnets/29 .html.

[7]Haidt, "Elevation and the Positive Psychology of Morality," p. 282.

[8]In Hebrew, *tikkun olam.*

[9]T. S. Eliot, "The Dry Salvages," in *Four Quartets* (San Diego: Harcourt Brace, 1943), line 33.

CONCLUSION: LIVING TOWARD COMPLETION

[1]Oliver Sachs, "The Joy of Old Age. (No Kidding)," *New York Times,* July 7, 2013, p. SR13.

[2]See Sigmund Freud, "Civilization and Its Discontents", in *The Standard Edition of the Complete Psychological Works of Sigmund Freud,* ed. James Strachey (1930; London: Hogarth, 1956-74), 21:101.

[3]See, for example, Augustine, "Ever Ancient, Ever New," http://feastofsaints .com/ancientnew.htm.

[4]Quoted by Philip Yancey in *Prayer: Does It Make Any Difference?* (Grand Rapids: Zondervan, 2006), p. 13.

[5]William Shakespeare, *Hamlet,* act 1, scene 5, lines 166-67.

[6]For a philosophical reflection on "fullness" as a constant possibility and hope throughout human history, see Charles Taylor's *Sources of the Self: The Making of Modern Identity* (Cambridge: Harvard University Press, 1989).

Index

About the Author

**Susan S. Phillips** (PhD) is executive director and professor of sociology and Christianity at New College Berkeley, an affiliate of the Graduate Theological Union dedicated to Christian education and spiritual formation for everyday life. In addition to teaching for New College Berkeley, she is a member of the faculty of the Diploma in the Art of Spiritual Direction program at San Francisco Theological Seminary and regularly teaches courses in spiritual theology at Fuller Theological Seminary (Menlo Park, California) and Regent College (Vancouver, British Columbia). In addition to teaching, Susan enjoys getting to know people as a spiritual director, retreat leader and speaker. Her books include *Candlelight: Illuminating the Art of Spiritual Direction* and *The Crisis of Care: Affirming and Restoring Caring Practices in the Helping Professions* (with Patricia Benner). She serves on the editorial boards of *Radix* and *Presence* magazines and the journal *Reflective Practice*. Susan is an elder at First Presbyterian Church of Berkeley, and she and her husband Steve are the blessed parents of Andrew and Peter. Visit her website at susanphillips.com.

formatio
TRADITION. EXPERIENCE.
TRANSFORMATION.

Formatio books from InterVarsity Press follow the rich tradition of the church in the journey of spiritual formation. These books are not merely about being informed, but about being transformed by Christ and conformed to his image. Formatio stands in InterVarsity Press's evangelical publishing tradition by integrating God's Word with spiritual practice and by prompting readers to move from inward change to outward witness. InterVarsity Press uses the chambered nautilus for Formatio, a symbol of spiritual formation because of its continual spiral journey outward as it moves from its center. We believe that each of us is made with a deep desire to be in God's presence. Formatio books help us to fulfill our deepest desires and to become our true selves in light of God's grace.